Everyday Applications Psychological Science

Everyday Applications of Psychological Science explores several core areas of psychology, showing readers how to apply these principles to everyday situations in order to better their understanding of human behavior and improve their quality of life.

The authors of this book, who are award-winning educators of psychology, have culled and collated the best practical research-based advice that psychological science can offer in an easy-to-read and digestible format. Lively and peppered with anecdotes, we explore topical areas normally found in introductory psychology books but do so in a way that makes psychological science practical, accessible, and relevant to our readers. In *Everyday Applications of Psychological Science*, the best science that psychology has to offer is translated into life hacks that are applicable to improving readers' physical health, mental health, psychological wealth, relationships, and happiness.

Everyday Applications of Psychological Science is vital reading for those interested in learning more about the field of psychology more generally and how aspects of psychological science can be applied to daily life. Our approach may be of particular interest to current and prospective undergraduate students of psychology and those interested in learning more about mental health issues.

R. Eric Landrum, PhD, is the Department Chair and a professor of Psychological Science at Boise State University, Boise, Idaho, United States. He served as president of Psi Chi, the International Honors Society in Psychology, and of the Society for Teaching Psychology. He was the 2019 recipient of the Charles L. Brewer Distinguished Teaching of Psychology Award for Distinguished Career in Teaching Psychology.

Regan A. R. Gurung, PhD, is the Associate Vice Provost and Executive Director of the Center for Teaching and Learning and a professor of Psychological Science at Oregon State University, Corvallis, OR, United States. He served as president of Psi Chi, the International Honors Society in Psychology, and of the Society for Teaching Psychology. He was the 2017 recipient of the Charles L. Brewer Award for Distinguished Career in Teaching Psychology.

Susan A. Nolan, PhD, is a professor of Psychology at Seton Hall University, South Orange, NJ, United States. She served as president of the Society for the Teaching of Psychology and of the Eastern Psychological Association. She was the 2020 recipient of the Fukuhara Award for Advanced International Research and Service from the International Council of Psychologists.

Maureen A. McCarthy, PhD, is the Dean of the College of Sciences and Humanities and a professor of Psychological Science at Ball State University, Muncie, IN, United States. She previously served as the president of the Society for the Teaching of Psychology.

Dana S. Dunn, PhD, is Professor of Psychology at Moravian University in Bethlehem, PA, United States. Earlier, he served as the president of the Society for the Teaching of Psychology, the Eastern Psychological Association, and Division 22 (Rehabilitation Psychology) of the American Psychological Association. He was the 2013 recipient of the Charles L. Brewer Award for Distinguished Career in Teaching Psychology.

Everyday Applications of Psychological Science
Hacks to Happiness and Health

R. Eric Landrum, Regan A. R. Gurung, Susan A. Nolan, Maureen A. McCarthy, and Dana S. Dunn

Routledge
Taylor & Francis Group

NEW YORK AND LONDON

Cover image: Getty

First published 2022
by Routledge
605 Third Avenue, New York, NY 10158

and by Routledge
4 Park Square, Milton Park, Abingdon, Oxon, OX14 4RN

Routledge is an imprint of the Taylor & Francis Group, an informa business

Library of Congress Cataloging-in-Publication Data
A catalog record for this title has been requested

ISBN: 978-1-032-03729-5 (hbk)
ISBN: 978-1-032-03725-7 (pbk)
ISBN: 978-1-003-18871-1 (ebk)

DOI: 10.4324/9781003188711

Typeset in Goudy
by Newgen Publishing UK

For those who see psychology as a way to improve their lives and the world we share.

Contents

Section 4 My relationships   93

Section 5 In closing: My happiness   117

Introduction

Fusion, Hybrid, Amalgam. These are terms that none of the authors of this book would use to describe this book. Those terms are catchy, trendy, popular, perhaps considered hip – that was not our goal in writing this book. Our goal, plain yet not so simple, was to extract the best science that psychology has to offer and translate it into life hacks that are applicable to improving your physical health, your mental health, your psychological wealth, your relationships, and your happiness. This is a relatively short book that is readable (we used endnotes[1] like this rather than APA-style in-text citations) and affordable. In our spare time, we like leaping tall buildings in a single bound.

This book can be what you make of it. Is it meant to be a comprehensive introduction to psychology, like you would see in a high school or college course? Not really. Could this be useful in such a course? Absolutely. We've worked hard to stay true to evidence-informed advice about these critical areas of all of our lives. Could someone get some real tips on how to improve their life, or how to help someone in trouble by reading this book? Yes. Psychology is the scientific study of the brain and behavior. That's big, in that it's a large area of study, from the smallest molecules of neurotransmitters that float the synaptic cleft to the largest macro environments of cultures and societies. Psychology encompasses who we were, who we are, who we can become, and who we will become. That *is* big.

Because the depth and breadth of psychology is indeed that deep and that wide, it is really not possible for one individual to know and remember all of the science that is known about human behavior. Given that we cannot know all, the logical question that follows is this: What should we know, and why? Are there basic facts about psychological science that everyone could benefit from knowing? I suppose you could Google certain questions about relationships or mental health, but the search results would provide hundreds of thousands of links to available information. As scientists and authors, we've read the studies and we've interpreted the data, and we can provide advice based on the best data currently available to us. *That* is a service that Google does not provide, and it is why authors still write books and why folks like you still read them.

If you think about this critically (and we hope that you are often a critical thinker), this may strike you as entirely subjective – five psychology professors,

DOI: 10.4324/9781003188711-1

plucked at random, to comment on essential concepts, ideas, and applications when introducing key psychological areas to a wide audience. First, note that there was no randomness at all. All of these contributors are high-achieving individuals at the top of the teaching of psychology field, each full-time professors at their respective universities (and at the time of writing this particular sentence, lacking humility too). Second, and this is a unique distinction indeed, they have all served as President of the Society for the Teaching of Psychology (STP), which is Division Two of the American Psychological Association – this is the largest association of teachers of psychology in the English-speaking world.

Third, this is a collaboration about telling the story of psychology, but the partnership is among the dearest of friends. Among the five of us, we bring you over 800 years of teaching experience in communicating psychological science (OK, now we're just checking to see if you are still reading, and if you are applying any of those critical thinking skills here). We purposely chose to write a book that would excite you about the story of psychology and provide useful information to help improve your life, but we did not want to offer the encyclopedic tome of 900 pages and 2,000 vocabulary terms. What if we were just to center on major, meaningful themes, and offer some life hacks – that was the goal of this collaboration. Our publishing partner Routledge supported this notion even further, and by encouraging us to stay within a word limit which would also help keep the price of this book down. Honestly, the lower the price, the more people the story will reach, and since we believe that these psych hacks can truly work to promote physical health, mental health, psychological wealth, relationships, and happiness, a greater chance at distribution is certainly worth a lower cost to our readers.

We should be fair and let you know that there are other means by which writers and readers could make decisions about what is "important" to share with an audience. We used our experience in the field to cherry-pick topics that we believe benefit the greatest number of people; we did not attempt here to write a replacement textbook for the introductory psychology course. For many years there have been multiple research efforts that asked faculty members to rate and rank the core terms in introductory psychology,[2,3,4,5] and that work continues somewhat today.[6] The introductory psychology course often gets attention from national education policymakers due to its size and scope; in recent years task forces and working groups have issued reports about the course, including the pillars model.[7] And although no one knows for sure (a crystal ball could be useful here), the typical estimate for the annual enrollment of introductory psychology students each year in the United States is between 1.2 million and 1.6 million students.[8] That would be an attractive audience, and if you are looking for a book in that area, we would certainly recommend the book co-authored by our very own beloved co-author, Susan Nolan.[9]

We hope that this text will satisfy the emergent triple-threat as articulated above: (1) the content of psychology is important and can be life-changing; (2) the assembled author team are expert teachers, researchers, and writers ready to deliver; and (3) the approach of sharing these psychological life hacks is just what the doctors ordered regarding understanding, comprehending, and applying the key principles of psychology to one's daily life. We have organized our thoughts about psych hacks into five different areas, and each is described briefly here.

My physical health

In this section, we present some of the critical details for maintaining your physical health, as if you had your own health psychologist giving you advice. From reviewing the details about health and stress, the biology that you need to know is presented (not a comprehensive review – for that, think about biology classes). Coping skills are vital for all of us, and to be successful, it's crucial to understand how these psychological processes work, whether that focus is on increasing health behavior or fighting sickness. All of the advice here is evidence-informed, and highly readable so that you can use it and develop psych hacks that are relevant for you and will work for you.

My mental health

In this section, we present many of the most popular topics when individuals are new to studying psychology. The entire notion of what is "normal" versus what is "abnormal" is a fascinating topic, and the impact of psychological disorders and mental illness in the United States is staggering. Rather than provide an encyclopedic overview of every possible mental disorder (for that, an undergraduate abnormal psychology course is the place to start), we present some key psychological disorders, along with some common treatment approaches. This section concludes with incredibly practical psych hacks about what to do if you think you need to seek therapy, and if someone you know is thinking about considering suicide, advice for what you should do. Literally a *life* hack!

My wealth

In this section, we present the key factors from psychological science about living a good life – what leads us to fulfillment? Although money is part of that equation, there are costs associated with being too money-centered. The notion of flourishing is to find happiness, satisfaction, and feelings of goodness in life. Working toward enrichment can mean avoiding the traps of materialism as well as cultivating one's beneficial qualities and practicing self-regulation. Psychological wealth is complex, and there are opportunities for enrichment that surround us in everyday life, whether they be appreciating the outdoors or strategic investments in time well spent. Enrichment also comes through our connections with others, and an important psych hack is the ability and interest to invest in yourself.

My relationships

In this section, we address some of the most important topics of all of our lives – how we interact with and get along with others. Humans are innately social beings, and our relationships are at the core of our existence. The challenges of successful relationships vary widely and often change over time, ranging from loneliness to partnering to breaking up to developing new relationships. We present the data about the benefits of healthy marriages and the detriments of unhealthy marriages. There are important workplace relationships to navigate for most of our adult lives, and we provide information and psych hacks that can be helpful here too. Thankfully, outcomes from psychological science allow us to conclude that relationships and social support are antidotes for success.

My happiness

As the concluding part of this introductory section, the "My Happiness" section is the "closer" for us – we attempt to tie it all together here. Happiness as a life outcome and goal is addressed throughout the book, but our final focus is squarely on happiness. In the psychological literature, it's called subjective well-being, but our knowledge base is broad – it's helpful to know what is linked to happiness, that is, individuals can gain insights and develop their own happiness hacks. There are interesting perspectives about the ability to manufacture and create happiness, and while it is known that good health leads to increased happiness, there is now experimental evidence that happiness can cause good health (yes, the *cause* word is appropriate here). Ultimately, we believe that a greater knowledge of psychology can lead to the potential for a happier and healthier life, or as we say, psych hacks.

It should be obvious by now that your authors have a specific lens or approach to the disciplinary nature of their work: psychological science. Furthermore, it is that the application of the principles of psychology (psych hacks) can be used to improve people's lives. One does not have to go to college and become a psychology major, take an introductory psychology course, or see a therapist to benefit from the discipline of psychology – although those three ideas mentioned here could be perfectly appropriate for you in a particular life situation.

We believe there is relevance to what we do, and we are sharing that with you in this book. For some individuals, the September 11, 2001, terrorist attacks in the United States changed the way we look at the world. During his year as American Psychological Association president in 2002, Philip Zimbardo[10] wrote the following about that important time:

> Even before the September 11th tragedy, most of the major problems facing the United States were psychological in cause, correlates, or consequence: for example, AIDS and sexually transmitted diseases; drug addiction, as

well as addictions to smoking, gambling, alcohol, and food; prejudice and discrimination; delinquency; violent crimes; educational failures for too many minority youth; and the full range of physical illnesses that are influenced by lifestyle and behavioral functioning. Psychologists have much to say about more effective ways of dealing with these problems at both individual and community levels of action. Psychologists need to be heard and to be at the table of influential leaders and policymakers because psychologists have more to say about these issues than do members of any other discipline.

(p. 432)

When thinking about the sections and the psych hacks presented throughout this book, the undergirding principle is that psychology is a science, and that psychological knowledge is gathered using the scientific method and advances in our knowledge are made using the same standards of evidence in any of the other sciences. This book is not meant to provide the entire context of how psychological researchers conduct research and draw conclusions – some of your authors have written those books too.[11,12]

But just to make this point, please consider the following listing of logical fallacies (with examples) that we fall prey to at times, reminding us how difficult it is to draw meaningful conclusions and how valuable it is when others follow the scientific method and publish peer-reviewed research studies advancing our knowledge base, slowly yet surely. Errors in the logic of an argument are called **logical fallacies,** and these typically stem from unreasoned argument, irrelevant distractions, or the absence of evidence.[13,14] We have presented here a partial listing of logical fallacies garnered from multiple sources.[15,16] As you read through them, think about how scientific findings could be corrupted by those who utilize logical fallacies, whether accidentally or purposefully. Also, think about how these approaches are used in the media, in advertising, by politicians, perhaps by your employer, or even by loved ones. Sometimes when we attempt to convince or persuade, we don't play fair, or we don't even try to play fair if we want what we want. It's important for all of us to understand these logical fallacies (even if we don't know their actual labels) and recognize that the arguments being made have flaws.

Ad hominem: Instead of inspecting the logic of the argument, the arguer launches a person attack instead; sometimes called "poisoning the well;" attacking the person rather than attacking the idea.

Appeal to tradition: An idea or event is "right" because it has always been done that way (sometimes referred to as "if it ain't broke, don't fix it"); this is often a way to squelch new or innovative ideas.

Argument from authority: This occurs when using expert opinion instead of using the evidence that the expert used to form his/her opinion; experts often talk about topics that are outside their realm of expertise; finding a "big name" to be on one's side of an argument who may not know anything about the topic.

Bandwagon fallacy: When the arguer believes that an idea or position has merit because a large number of other people also believe in the idea or position. Large numbers of followers do not necessarily make an argument believable just based on the large numbers; popular does not equal right or just.

Blood is thicker than water: When an argument is automatically accepted as true if stated by someone who is related to the arguer or who knows/ likes the arguer; also called favoritism or "for my friends, anything" – this actually is a shortcut to actually thinking, as someone who is related may not be making a logical argument.

Circular argument: When the argument is restated without the provision of proof, such as "the President is a great communicator due to the fact that he speaks effectively," or "we know that God exists because God exists." Sometimes this is called "begging the question" – this is often used when the person does not have external evidence to support a claim, but wants others to accept the claim on its face.

Guilt by association: The arguer commits this fallacy when linking the person (or person's argument) to a group that may be perceived as negative by some or many, such as "don't follow his advice, because he used to work as an ambulance-chaser type of attorney" – this is a dangerous argument because it relies on stereotypes, meaning that one member of a group possesses all the stereotypical characteristics of that group, rather than considering the person as a unique individual.

Non sequitur: When the arguer makes an inappropriate leap from the evidence provided to the conclusion, such as the number of homicides increasing when there is a high tide in the ocean. The tide and the number of homicides may be statistically related, but that does not necessarily mean they are causally related. Events can be spuriously correlated (shoe size and IQ might be positively correlated), but that does not mean that one causes the other.

Paralysis of analysis: This is the belief that since we will never have all the data, it's too early to make a decision and that actions should be delayed until later; this has been a popular argument in the climate change debate for decades, or even with individuals who do not have all of the options known to them so they end up remaining with the status quo.

Post hoc ergo propter hoc: This occurs when the arguer assumes that the temporal precedence explains cause and effect, such as "after I ate the steak at the restaurant, I got sick, which means the steak made me sick" – humans often want to assert causality to events that A caused B but just because A happened before B, that is not a causal link necessarily; this is a jump to conclusions.

Red herring: This is a tactic that is used to divert attention away from the main argument, such as "the logging of the Pacific Northwest may be bad for the environment, but what will the workers in the paper mills do to support their families?" – think of this as the magician doing a trick that gets you to look one direction while the "magic" is happening in another direction; distraction can lead to the derailment of a meaningful discussion.

Reductionism: When the arguer answers a complex question with a simple answer, in the context that the audience may not perceive how complicated the situation is; also called oversimplifying; individuals do this all the time, such as politicians who want to end welfare programs and mandate mandatory part-time employment for those on welfare; the one-line sound bite may be catchy to some, but the actual situation and life conditions are so complicated that there is no easy answer and the solution cannot be reduced to one size fits all.

Slippery slope: This is the argument that if Event 1 happens, then Event 2 will happen, then Event 3, ... then Event 16, and so on. We don't want Event 16 to happen, so we don't want Event 1 to start us sliding down the slippery slope. This is another distraction technique that is used to avoid the discussion of the core issues, such as if we stop enforcing the high school dress code, students will make poor clothing choices, then there will be more envy between teenagers, then there will be clothing theft from lockers, so changing the school dress code will result in more vandalism (ah, the slippery slope).

Testimonial: When someone who is well-known (but not an expert) provides an endorsement for a product or an idea, such as a famous athlete urging voters to vote for a particular candidate; paid testimonials may be additionally suspect – this is the essence of much of modern commercial advertising, celebrity endorsements on social media, fundraising campaigns all over the world, and so on. Personal stories are memorable, persuasive, and can evoke powerful emotions and behaviors.

As you read this book and think about these logical fallacies, a psych hack for you to develop is to not fall prey to these concepts – recognize them when they occur and try to not let them influence your behavior negatively.

Although it's not one of our explicit goals in this book, along the way you may realize that you start to develop some skills in the area of psychological literacy – or perhaps you are expanding your existing skills. This notion of **psychological literacy** and the idea of a psychological literate citizen is again in the forefront of our disciplinary consciousness.[17] In this work, psychological literacy is defined as:

- having a well-defined vocabulary and basic knowledge of the critical subject matter in psychology;
- valuing the intellectual challenges required to use scientific thinking and the disciplined analysis of information to evaluate alternative courses of action;
- taking a creative and amiable skeptic approach to problem solving;

- applying psychological principles to personal, social, and organizational issues at work, relationships, and the broader community;
- acting ethically;
- being competent in using and evaluating information and technology;
- communicating effectively in different modes and with many different audiences;
- recognizing, understanding, and fostering respect for diversity; and
- being insightful and reflective about one's own and others' behavior and mental processes.

(p. 11)

By reading this book, you will not be able to achieve all of the skills listed here; that would likely take pursuing a bachelor's degree in psychology. However, many of the psych hacks we offer throughout this book are indeed represented in some way in this list. We believe that you will come away with evidence-informed psych hacks that you can use to improve your life and those around you. It should be a fun adventure written by teachers of psychology at the top of their profession who care passionately about sharing the pro tips for your health, wealth, relationships, and happiness. We're psychological scientists and we're here to help.

Notes

1 This is an example of an endnote. Ideally, it will make the text easier for you to read than interrupting the text with a citation that would look like this (Landrum, Gurung, Nolan, McCarthy, & Dunn, 2022).

2 Boneau, C. A. (1990). Psychological literacy: A first approximation. *American Psychologist, 45*(7), 891–900.

3 Landrum, R. E. (1993). Identifying core concepts in introductory psychology. *Psychological Reports, 72*(2), 659–666.

4 Quereshi, M. Y. (1993). The contents of introductory psychology textbooks: A follow-up. *Teaching of Psychology, 20*(4), 218–222.

5 Zechmeister, J. S., & Zechmeister, E. B. (2000). Introductory psychology textbooks and psychology's core concepts. *Teaching of Psychology, 27*(1), 6–11.

6 Griggs, R. A., & Bates, S. C. (2014). Topical coverage in introductory psychology: Textbooks versus lectures. *Teaching of Psychology, 41*(2), 144–147. https://doi.org/10.1177/0098628314530347

7 Gurung, R. A. R., Hackathorn, J., Enns, C., Frantz, S., Cacioppo, J. T., Loop, T., & Freeman, J. E. (2016). Strengthening introductory psychology: A new model for teaching the introductory course. *American Psychologist, 71*(2), 112–124. https://doi.org/10.1037/a0040012

8 Steuer, F. B., & Ham, K. W., II. (2008). Psychology textbooks: Examining their accuracy. *Teaching of Psychology, 35*(3), 160–168. https://doi.org/10.1080/00986280802189197

9 Hockenbury, S. E., & Nolan, S. A. (2019). *Discovering psychology* (8th ed.). Macmillan Learning.

10 Zimbardo, P. G. (2002). Psychology in the public service. *American Psychologist, 57*(6–7), 431–433. https://doi.org/10.1037/0003-066X.57.6-7.431

11 Dunn, D. S. (2018). *Research methods for social psychology* (2nd ed.). Wiley.

12 Beins, B. C., & McCarthy, M. A. (2018). *Research methods and statistics in psychology* (2nd ed.). Cambridge University Press.

13 Hahn, U. (2011). The problem of circularity in evidence, argument, and explanation. *Perspectives in Psychological Science, 6*(2), 172–182. https://doi.org/10.1177/1745691611400240

14 Weber, R., & Brizee, A. (2013). *Logical fallacies*. Purdue Online Writing Laboratory. http://owl.english.purdue.edu/owl/resource/659/03/

15 Weber & Brizee (2013).

16 Williamson, O. M. (2006). *Master list of logical fallacies*. University of Texas at El Paso. http://utminers.utep.edu/omwilliamson/ENGL1311/fallacies.htm

17 McGovern, T. V., Corey, L., Cranney, J., Dixon, W. E., Jr., Holmes, J. D., Kuebli, J. E., … Walker, S. J. (2010). Psychologically literate citizens. In D. F. Halpern (Ed.), *Undergraduate education in psychology: A blueprint for the future of the discipline* (pp. 9–27). American Psychological Association.

Section 1   My physical health

Would you like a concise list stating what you need to do to be healthy? You probably know most of it already – eat nutritious meals, get physical activity, don't smoke, don't get stressed out. Easier said than done. We may know what we *need* to do, but it is a completely different thing to *actually do it*. The great news is that findings from years of psychological research can help us do each of these different healthy behaviors better. If you ask people what they most want, "money" may be a common answer (more on this in sections on that topic), but "healthy" and "happy" are often on the top of the list. Here, we focus on many of the ways you can be physically healthy.

Part 1.1   What is being healthy anyway?

Whereas a large part of our psychological mind space can be taken up by the fear of death, people consciously and unconsciously tend to want to live long, healthy, and happy lives. People buy personal health trackers such as Fitbits to exercise more though researchers show it may not lead to weight loss.[1] Every January gym membership jumps and home fitness equipment is lugged to basements to hit those New Year resolutions. We try to eat more of what is good for us. Sometimes we pop pills engineered to boost our immune systems or replenish missing elements in our diet. It is great to be alive, and being healthy helps us maximize the joys of living. Health is a complex blend of biological, psychological, and societal factors. What can you do to optimize your health? What does psychological science tell us about being healthy? The first key step to staying alive longer, healthier, and happier is getting a clear sense of what "health" is.

Health is best defined as a state of complete physical, mental, and social well-being.[2] This broad definition is especially useful because it includes the mental component, which is particularly susceptible to psychological pressures from situations around us. One way to see health is as a continuum, with optimal health (broadly defined) at one end and poor health at the other. The number of healthy things we do in life determines our relative position on the continuum (closer to optimal health or closer to death) at a particular moment in time. The healthy things we do (eat and sleep well, exercise, take time to relax) move us toward the optimal health side. The unhealthy things we do

DOI: 10.4324/9781003188711-2

(eat junk food, get stressed, smoke, drink excessively) make us slide toward the illness side. Of course, not everything can be compensated for. If you have smoked for 20 or 30 years, it is pretty hard to slide to the healthy other end. Furthermore, it is difficult to compare the extent to which different behaviors translate into longevity. Just because you do not smoke does not mean that you can drink excessively. Just because you exercise a lot does not mean you can afford to not eat a nutritious diet. Keeping your life moving toward optimal health is a daily challenge and a dynamic process, both strongly influenced by social psychological factors.[3]

The challenge to achieve optimal health is made more difficult by the interaction of nature and culture. Many times, nature pushes us in one direction but our cultural background or the rules of the culture we are embedded in push us in another. Our evolutionary history shows, for example, that we are all biologically wired to crave and enjoy fatty and salty foods. The tendency to eat as much fat and salt as we like, and consequently to grow heavier, runs into the cultural ideals of health and fitness we see in the media. Smokers with a nicotine addiction may want to light up a cigarette whenever they are out in public, but cultural smoking bans prevent them from doing so. Sometimes culture can work in the opposite direction as well. For example, in countries such as India and Japan, smoking is still normative as compared to North America. Although the urge to smoke is not a natural, innate urge, someone growing up in a culture where many people smoke may be more likely to smoke as well. Families are often such cultural settings, and young children are very likely to eat as well and be as physically active as their parents.

It was not until the early 20th century that psychology started to play a part in the examination of health. We now have a good set of #psychhacks because of early psychologists such as Freud, Alexander, and Dubar and organizations such as the Society for Health Psychology and the Society for Behavioral Medicine. For the past 50 plus years, health psychologists used the methods of psychology to examine health. Within mainstream psychology, researchers in social psychology, personality psychology, cognitive psychology, and clinical psychology realized that the basic theories that they derived to describe and predict behavior could be used in the study of health and well-being. The following sections give you some key life hacks based on this research.

Part 1.2 Get stressed much?

Why do different people experience stress differently? What can we do to reduce stress? If you can get a good handle on dealing with stress, that is perhaps the best #psychhack to know of. Stress is a word we use often, but there are some significant variations in how it is defined, how it is studied, and everyone has a different notion of what is stressful. It is useful to have a specific definition of stress which can be applied to many different people (and animals too).

All negative events need not be stressful, and all positive events are not automatically free from stress. For example, losing your job may sound initially like a stressful event, but it may be a happy event if you hated your job. Similarly, although finding a romantic partner after a long period of being single sounds very positive, you may worry about how to make sure it lasts. As you can see, stress is subjective. What, then, is a convenient way to define stress? This is a good time to assess your own stress, using the questionnaire in Table 1.1.

Most researchers contend that the best way to know when a person is stressed is to look at how the person's body responds to a situation. If the sympathetic nervous system activates in response to an event, then the person is under stress. This results in elevated heart rate, respiration, and circulation. Many early definitions of stress relied heavily on biological activity. Cannon[4] viewed stress as the biological mobilization of the body for action, involving sympathetic activation and endocrine activity. Selye[5] similarly viewed stress as

Table 1.1 Some of the major stressors as assessed by the Hassles scales

1. Death of a close family member	100
2. Death of a close friend	73
3. Divorce between parents	65
4. Jail term	63
5. Major personal injury	63
6. Marriage	58
7. Fired from job	50
8. Failed important course	47
9. Change in health of a family member	45
10. Pregnancy	44
11. Sex problems	44
12. Serious argument with family member	40
13. Change in financial status	39
14. Change of major	39
15. Trouble with parents	39
16. New girl or boy friend	38
17. Increased workload at school	37
18. Outstanding personal achievement	36
19. First semester in college	35
20. Change in living conditions	31
21. Serious argument with instructor	30
22. Lower grades than expected	29
23. Change in sleeping habits	29
24. Change in social habits	29
25. Change in eating habits	28
26. Chronic car trouble	26
27. Change in number of family get-togethers	26
28. Too many missed classes	25
29. Change of college	24
30. Dropped more than one class	23
31. Minor traffic violations	20

On the scale, you can determine your "stress score" by adding up the number of points corresponding to the events that you have experienced in the past six months or expect to experience in the coming six months.

the activation of a host of physiological systems. We will give you what all the physiology you need to understand this in a bit. More psychological theories defined stress as being caused when the perceived demands on the organism exceeded the resources to meet those demands.[1]

Although these different definitions have all been well supported, the simplest definition of **stress** is the upsetting of homeostasis.[9] Our bodies have an optimal level of functioning in regard to blood sugar level, body temperature, rate of circulation, and breathing. **Homeostasis** is the ideal level of bodily functions. Similar to the thermostat in homes, our body is designed to maintain its optimal level in all areas of functioning. We set our thermostats and if the temperature drops below the set level, the furnace starts. In this way a constant temperature is maintained. The hypothalamus in our brains similarly maintains set levels. Stress to our systems can thus be seen as something that upsets our ideal balance.

This simple but effective definition of stress harkens back to the origins of the word *stress*. Physicists long studied the effects of large forces on solid structures, and *stress* was originally used to describe the force exerted on a body that resulted in deformation or strain. Stress has similar effects on our body. This definition allows for subjectivity, as stressors can vary across individuals. If an event does not activate your stress response or disrupt your system, it is just another event. If an event disrupts you, it is a stressor. One person's event can be another person's stressor. For example, talking in public may not be stressful for you, but it could be very stressful for someone else. Four major psychological theories expand on this basic understanding of stress. But first, some critical physiology.

Part 1.3 The biological secrets you need to know

Understanding the physiological bases of stress provides us with a better understanding of how psychology can make a difference. Even if you are or were anti-biology, you will appreciate getting a refresher on some basics as they make the psychological aspects make more sense. A simple meditation task works on your mind (i.e., cognitions) and your body (i.e., physiology). We will leave some of you salivating for more biology (sorry).

The nervous system is the most critical physiological player although its functioning also influences the endocrine system together with which it supervises the functioning of the cardiovascular system, the respiratory system, the digestive system, and the reproductive system. No reproduction in this section. No digestion either. For stress, the nervous system is key and bears a little more in-depth understanding.

The nervous system can be divided into two main parts: The **central nervous system** (CNS) (consisting of the brain and spinal cord) and the **peripheral nervous system** (consisting of all the nervous tissue and cells outside the brain and spinal cord). The primary function of the CNS is to process and coordinate information that it receives from the peripheral nervous system. In essence, the CNS is the command center of the body with the brain as the main coordinator. The brain coordinates every aspect of the stress response. In addition, the "psychological" part of health psychology has its physiological basis in different parts of the brain.

Our brain can be divided into three main parts. The hindbrain or rhomben-cephalon is located at the back of the brain and consists of the medulla, pons, and cerebellum. The medulla controls life-support functions (e.g., breathing), the pons relays information from the spinal cord to the higher brain areas, and the cerebellum controls motor coordination and movement in response to sensory stimuli. The midbrain or mesencephalon consists of structures that process visual information (superior colliculus) and auditory information (inferior colliculus) and those that play a key role in attention, pain control, and emotions (tegmentum, periaqueductal gray, and substantia nigra). The reticular formation plays a key role in the stress response handling emergency responses. It is a group of neurons that takes up a large portion of the midbrain but runs from the hindbrain to the forebrain.

The forebrain or prosencephalon is the part of the brain that you most likely associate with the word **brain**, that bean-shaped structure with grooves and fissures. This is the area where all that makes us human resides. Thinking, consciousness, talking, eating, and creating are all functions housed in the fore-brain. Most of what you see or picture is only the cerebral cortex, the surface lobes of the brain. The cortex consists of four lobes. The frontal lobe contains the motor cortex and key command centers for the body. The parietal lobe processes sensory data from the body. The temporal lobe processes auditory, smell, and taste information. The occipital lobe processes visual information.

Under the cerebral cortex are other key forebrain structures. Perhaps the single most influential part of the brain is located in the forebrain. The hypo-thalamus directly controls the activity of the pituitary gland, which releases hormones and correspondingly regulates all of our motivated behaviors. Just above the hypothalamus (*hypo* means *below* just like hypodermic needle means penetrating below the skin) lies the thalamus, which relays informa-tion from the brain stem all over the cerebral cortex. The temporal lobe houses the hippocampus and amygdala, two structures making up what is called the limbic system. The hippocampus plays a pivotal role in emotions and memory, and the amygdala produces fear, escape, rage, and aggression. Many of these structures will feature prominently in the first major stress theory we discuss.

The spinal cord extends from the base of the skull to the tailbone and in cross-section resembles a gray "X." The gray matter consists of cell bodies of neurons and is surrounded by bundles of white axons. Bundles of axons are referred to as tracts (in the CNS) and nerves (in the peripheral nervous system). Bundles of cell bodies are referred to as nuclei (in the CNS) and gan-glia (in the peripheral nervous system). Sensory information from the periph-eral nervous system travels up the tracts in the CNS to the brain.

The peripheral nervous system transmits information to the entire body with 12 pairs of cranial nerves and 31 pairs of spinal nerves (one pair leaving the spinal cord at each of the vertebra in our spines). The two nerves com-prising a pair serve each side of the body. The peripheral nervous system has two main divisions, the somatic nervous system and the autonomic nervous system. The somatic nervous system controls the skeletal muscles and is under conscious control. You can decide to move your arm to prop this book up higher, and then you can do it. The autonomic nervous system coordinates muscles not under your voluntary control and acts automatically in response to signals from the CNS. Your heart muscles, for example, are under autonomic control. One signal from the hypothalamus can lead to your heart rate jumping up. Another signal can make it slow down. An arm of the autonomic system called the **sympathetic nervous system** (SNS) produces the speeding up responses. Another arm of the system known as the **parasympathetic nervous system** (PNS) produces the slowing down responses. We talk a lot more about these two arms of the autonomic system in the context of stress below.

This basic physiology underlies all the different theories of stress. While the biological jargon and processes above may be the #psychhack to why you feel how you do when you get stressed, psychological science has developed four major explanations of the concept of "being stressed."

Part 1.4 Step behind the curtain of stress research

Being stressed is a psychological experience for all of us though it is accompanied by and perhaps you can say even driven by a whole host of physiological activity. You could argue that without some of that physiological activity there would be no stress, but that would be inaccurate. The bigger and scarier reality is that our psychological activity can drive our physiology and make us stressed. Not surprisingly, over close to 80 years of stress research has led to many theories as to how and why we get stressed. In this section, let's meet the four major ones.

The fight-or-flight response. Walter Cannon applied the concept of homeostasis to the study of human interactions with the environment.[6] The basic idea is intuitive and can be remembered by a simple example. Imagine finding yourself face to face with a bear freshly escaped from the local zoo. You can probably guess what your body will do. Your heart pumps faster, your blood pressure rises, you breathe faster, your face is a little flushed, and your palms may be sweaty. All these reactions are caused by the SNS that prepares your body for action. Activation of the SNS increases circulation, respiration, and metabolism, all factors that fuel your body to ready it to either fight the bear or flee, escaping as fast as you can. The higher respiration rate gets more oxygen into your lungs, the increased heart rate and blood pressure get the oxygenated blood to the muscles, and the increased metabolism breaks down energy for use by the fighting/fleeing muscles. The SNS also turns off certain systems in response to stress. Faced with a ravenous bear, you are probably not in a mood for food or sex. The SNS down regulates (turns off) the digestive system and the reproductive system in times of stress. The SNS activates the adrenal medulla, which secretes the major stress hormones adrenalin and noradrenalin (also called epinephrine and norepinephrine and collectively called the catecholamines) that stimulate the **fight-or-flight response.**

The reversal of this process (the activating of some systems and the deactivating of others), which helps your body recover from a stressor, is managed by the PNS. The PNS decreases circulation and respiration and increases digestion and reproduction. Correspondingly, most stress management techniques work toward activating your PNS and slowing down breathing and heart rate. The PNS and SNS are both parts of the autonomic nervous system and are coordinated by higher brain structures such as the hypothalamus.

General adaptation syndrome. Hans Selye chanced on a new way of understanding stress after he unintentionally mishandled his lab rats. Selye was not an experienced animal handler, and he had much trouble weighing, injecting, and studying his rats. Through different forms of (unintended) mistreatment, he stressed both the experimental and control groups, and both groups developed ulcers. The rats also showed other physiological changes, including shrunken adrenal glands and deformed lymph nodes.[10] On realizing the cause of the ulcers, Selye exposed rats to a variety of stressors such as extreme heat and cold, sounds, and rain. He found that in every case the rats developed physiological problems similar to those of the mistreated rats. Selye concluded that organisms must have a general, nonspecific response to a variety of stressful events. Specifically, he hypothesized that no matter what the stressor, the body would react in the same way, and theorized that these responses were driven by the hypothalamic–pituitary–adrenal (HPA) axis. The hypothalamus activates the pituitary gland, which then activates the adrenal gland, which then secretes the chemical cortisol.

Selye argued that organisms have a general way of responding to all stressors, which he called a **general adaptation syndrome**. When faced with a stressor – whether a wild animal, a threatening mugger, or intense cold – the body first goes into a state of alarm. HPA activation takes place, and the body attempts to cope with the stressor during a period of resistance. If the stressor persists for too long, the body breaks down in a state of exhaustion. Many acute or short-term stressors can be successfully dealt with in the resistance stage. Chronic or long-term stressors drive us to exhaustion. Chronic stressors can exert true physiological and psychological damage on human brains and bodies, making real the phrase "stress can kill."[7,8]

Cognitive appraisal model. Richard Lazarus[9] devised the first psychological model of stress, known as the **cognitive appraisal model**. Lazarus saw stress as an imbalance between the demands placed on the individual and that individual's resources to cope. He argued that the experience of stress differs significantly across individuals, depending on how they interpret the event and the outcome of a specific sequence of thinking patterns called **appraisals**.

All of us are faced with demands. In college, you have papers to write and exams to take. At work, you may have projects and production deadlines to meet or a certain number of sales to make. Even in our personal lives, our family and friends rely on us and expect us to do various things. These different expectations, deadlines, and situations are all potential stressors. However, according to Lazarus, these expectations, deadlines, and situations are just events until we *deem* them to be stressful. The main cognitive process at work here is that of making appraisals.

Lazarus suggested that we make two major types of appraisals when we face any potentially stressful event. During **primary appraisals**, we ascertain whether the event is positive, negative, or neutral, and if negative, whether it is harmful, threatening, or challenging. A *harm* (or harm-loss) appraisal is made when we expect to lose something of great personal significance. For example, when we break up a close relationship, we lose a confidant. The event may involve the loss of psychological aspects, such as support from an ex-partner or the love of a parent who is dying; harm to one's self-esteem with the loss of a job; or even physical harm and loss, as in the diagnosis of a terminal illness. *Threat* appraisals are made when we believe the event will be extremely demanding and will put us at risk for damage. If you think that your bad performance on an upcoming project can severely ruin your reputation or that taking part in a certain race will hurt your body, you are seeing the project or race as a threat. *Challenge* appraisals occur when we believe that we can grow as a result of dealing with the event or when we look at positive ways in which we can benefit from it. For example, you can view an exam as harmful to your self-esteem and a threat if you expect to do badly, or you can view it as a challenge to your intelligence and how much you have studied. A primary appraisal can be heavily influenced by the stake we have in the outcome of the event.[10]

After we make a primary appraisal, we assess whether or not we have the necessary resources to cope with the event. During *secondary appraisal*, we determine whether we can deal with the event and how we can cope. We may think about the social support we have, who can help us, and what exactly can be done. We are asking ourselves the question, "Do I have what it takes to cope?" If our answer is no, we do not have the resources to cope, and we have appraised the event as harmful or threatening, then we appraise the event as a stressor. If our answer is yes, and we have appraised the event as a challenge, the event remains just that – an event. Throughout this process, we often engage in cognitive reappraisal, changing how we view the situation.

Many factors contribute to the appraisals of events. The *duration* of an event can play an important role in the process. Acute or short-term events may be appraised differently from chronic or long-term events. You may not worry too much if you know that the loud noise outside your window will stop in minutes. You may have an entirely different reaction if you live under the flight path of a nearby airport. Events can be either *negative* or *positive*. This dimension of stress is more straightforward. Some events are automatically threatening on the surface, such as having to speak in front of 500 people or being chased by people you do not know. Others may be positive on the surface, such as getting married, but may involve a great many demands on your mind and body, such as planning the wedding.

Control is another important factor in stress. When you believe that you have control over a situation, the situation is less likely to be stressful. Knowing that you are capable of changing the event is less stressful than not having any control over it. Nursing home residents who got extra control over their day-to-day activities, such as menus and recreational activities, were significantly better off.[11] *Predictability* is also related to control. You will fear going to class less if you know that your professor gives a quiz every Friday. If you have no idea when a quiz will be given, you will probably be more stressed.

Tend and befriend. There are sex differences in stress responses: In addition to fighting or fleeing, women may **tend and befriend**.[12,13] Researchers noticed that diverse findings in the stress literature did not fit the fight-or-flight model. This model assumed that men and women faced the same challenges in our evolutionary history. However, this was not true. Females have always been primary caregivers of infants because of their greater investment in giving birth (nine months for women versus minutes for men) and ability to breast-feed. Men were able to fight or flee, but women often had to look after infants. If a woman fought and lost, she would leave her infant defenseless. If she ran, she would either have to leave her infant behind or the weight of the infant might slow her down and lead to capture. Instead, women developed additional stress responses aimed at protecting, calming, and quieting the child (tending) to remove it from harm's way and marshal resources to help.[17] Essentially, women create social networks to provide resources and protection for themselves and their infants (befriending). The tend-and-befriend response is thus a more rational stress response for females than the basic fight-or-flight response. This theory builds on the brain's attachment/caregiving system, which counteracts the metabolic activity associated with the traditional fight-or-flight stress response – increased heart rate, blood pressure, and cortisol levels – and leads to nurturing and affiliate behavior.

In clear support of the theory, researchers showed that after a stressful day on the job, men wanted to be left alone and often fought with their spouses and children.[14] When stressed, women, actually tended to spend more time with their children and have more physical contact with them.

Part 1.5 So how do you cope?

Great. You know the biology and psychology of why you get stressed. Now let's review how to cope with it. **Coping** is defined as individual efforts made to manage distressing problems and emotions that affect the physical and psychological outcomes of stress. If stress is a disturbance in homeostasis, coping is whatever we do to reestablish our homeostatic balances. It is tricky though. Remember that people and situations vary a lot. What may work for one person may not work for another. Similarly, what works in one situation may not work well in another. If that is not enough variability, what works for one person in one situation may not work for another person in the same situation. Coping includes anything people do to manage problems or emotional responses, whether successful or not.

The two most basic styles are **approach coping** and **avoidant coping**. An individual can approach a stressor and make active efforts to resolve it or try to avoid the problem. You can either do something about the problem or you can ignore it. Researchers have particularly distinguished between problem-focused or emotion-focused coping strategies.

Problem-focused coping involves directly facing the stressful situation and working hard to resolve it. For example, if you have a demanding, aggressive boss at work, you may experience a lot of stress at your job. If you report the issue to your human resources department or have a direct conversation with your boss, you are taking concrete action to deal with the situation and following a problem-focused approach.

Sometimes the first thing you do is deal with the emotions surrounding the stressor. A person finding out that he or she is COVID-19 positive or has test results showing cancer may experience a surge of fear and anxiety and is driven to cope with these feelings. The person may deny the test results or not want to talk about them for some time. This strategy of coping is referred to as **emotion-focused coping** because you use either mental or behavioral methods to deal with the feelings resulting from the stress. More often than not, problem-focused and emotion-focused styles are pitted against each other. Although conceptually distinct, both strategies are interdependent and work together, with one supplementing the other in the overall coping process.

It sounds like avoidant, emotion-focused coping may not be the best style, so is approach problem-solving coping the best? We wish. It really depends on the situation. There is over-reliance on the "problem-focused coping is good, emotion-focused coping is bad" dichotomy. It is essentially best to match the type of coping you use with the situation and with your comfort level. In the short term, avoidant, emotion-focused coping may be beneficial because this coping style gives your body time to recover from the shock of and physiological responses to the stressor. If you were diagnosed with cancer and you are so anxious that you cannot function, it may be better to be emotion-focused and first cope with your emotions and ignore the issue because it stresses you. At some point, however, you must face the problem, get more information about it, and learn what you should do to deal with it.

Some people cope with stress by buying and consuming a pint (or a gallon!) of their favorite ice cream. Others go for a fast run. Still others sleep extra hours and do not eat. You may have some friends or coworkers who are not fazed even when everything seems to be going wrong. Other individuals fall apart and get "freaked out" by the most minor negative events. According to Lazarus and Folkman's (1984) framework, cognitive appraisals and coping are two critical mediators of responses to stressful events. A person's subjective perception of stress will depend on the objective features of the situation (e.g., potentially stressful life events) and the way that person appraises the events. Your feeling of stress depends both on how many things you really have due and on how serious or demanding you think the assignments or deadlines are. Even if you do not really have too much to do, just believing that you have too much to do or that what you have to do is very difficult can be stressful. A person experiences distress when primary appraisals of threat exceed secondary appraisals of coping ability. One's secondary appraisal will depend in large part on the personal resources a person brings to the situation, such as personality factors (e.g., optimism) and perceived resources for coping with the situation. Many factors influence how someone appraises a situation and correspondingly copes with stress. In this section, we will examine some of the factors that influence appraisals and coping and make the difference between weathering the storm and falling to pieces.

Psychological processes at work. Some basic psychological theories also influence our behaviors when we are stressed and when we get ill. A person's personality characteristics provide some of the best clues as to how they will cope with a stressor. **Personality** is defined as an individual's unique set of consistent behavioral traits, where traits are durable dispositions to behave in a particular way in a variety of situations. A wealth of research suggests that personality can be sufficiently measured by assessing how conscientious, agreeable, neurotic, open to experience, and extraverted a person is – these are know as the 'Big Five' personality traits. Each trait, characteristics of the trait, and examples of each trait are listed in Table 1.2. We include more about the Big Five in Section 4 as well, in the context of relationships.

Some people's personality types make them attend more to bodily sensations and report more symptoms than others.[15] People who monitor their symptoms to an extreme may be **hypochondriacs**, constantly worried about their health. Hypochondriacs believe that any minor change in their condition could be the sign of a major problem. They are constantly going to doctors to be checked. Even when they are told they are all right, they do not believe the diagnosis and may change doctors.[16]

Personality traits such as optimism and self-esteem normally buffer us against stress and illness, but may also delay seeking treatment. People with high self-esteem believe that they are very healthy and are optimistic in their outlook. They may also believe that their bodies can fight off infections or heal without specific medical treatment. People high in optimism may even downplay the negative symptoms they experience and expect things to turn around shortly. These people may wait and see if they get better, but sometimes they wait too long.

It is probably no surprise that some personality types use different coping styles than others. For example, in a study of 298 outpatients with depression, those patients with less-adaptive coping strategies (i.e., emotion-focused coping) had less-adaptive personality traits (i.e., neuroticism) and were

Table 1.2 The Big Five personality traits

Trait	Characteristics
Conscientiousness	Ethical, dependable, productive, purposeful
Agreeableness	Sympathetic, warm, trusting, cooperative
Neuroticism	Anxious, insecure, guilt-prone, self-conscious
Openness to experience	Daring, nonconforming, imaginative
Extraversion	Talkative, sociable, fun-loving, affectionate

more depressed. The reverse was found for adaptive problem-focused coping strategies.[17]

Beyond these core aspects of personality, people vary on a number of other characteristics that can influence their coping. For example, health psychologists suggest that we pay close attention to the concepts of optimism, mastery, hardiness, and resilience. **Optimism** refers to generalized outcome expectancies that good things, rather than bad things, will happen. Optimists are the people who can always find the positive aspects of any situation and always seem to look on the bright side of life no matter how bad things are. This personality trait is associated with a number of health-related factors.

Mastery is a relatively stable tendency of an individual and another variable that can influence the appraisal of stress and help people cope. Mastery is defined as the extent to which one regards one's life chances as being under one's own control.[18] Someone with a high level of mastery believes that he or she has the capability to succeed at whatever task is at hand.

Two other personality characteristics that moderate the effects of stress and aid coping are hardiness and resilience. People who are strongly committed to their lives, enjoy challenges, and have a high level of control over their lives are high on the trait of **hardiness**. Resilience closely relates to hardiness. If you see a person who has encountered a tremendous number of stressful events but always seems to bounce back into action and still do fine is said to be resilient. Like hardiness, resiliency accompanies adaptive coping strategies that lead to better mental and physical health.

How we cope with stress often is influenced by how much support we receive from others around us. Even more importantly, just the perception that support would be available if we need it can greatly enhance our coping strategies. Not surprisingly then, social support is one of the most important factors in the study of stress and coping. **Social support**, generally defined as emotional, informational, or instrumental assistance from others has been tied to better health, more rapid recovery from illness, and a lower risk for mortality.

Assess your coping. Each of the two main styles discussed previously, problem-focused and emotion-focused coping, has many separate subcomponents, each of which can be assessed by questionnaires. One of the most commonly used measures is the Ways of Coping Questionnaire (WCQ).[19] The WCQ has 50 items (16 are fillers) measuring 8 main types of coping. See which of the following you use:

1   Confrontive Coping (e.g., I stood my ground and fought for what I wanted)
2   Distancing (e.g., I went on as if nothing had happened)
3   Self-Controlling (e.g., I tried to keep my feelings to myself)
4   Seeking Social Support (e.g., I talked to someone to find out more about the situation)
5   Accepting Responsibility (e.g., I criticized or lectured myself)
6   Escape Avoidance (e.g., I hoped a miracle would happen)
7   Planful Problem Solving (e.g., I made a plan of action and followed it)
8   Positive Reappraisal (e.g., I changed or grew as a person in a good way).

Try these to cope. There is a broad category of approaches called relaxation-based approaches that can help you cope. It includes a lot of usual suspects such as mindfulness, meditation, yoga, biofeedback, and hypnosis. The main goal is to reduce the number of thoughts you are experiencing and to activate the parasympathetic nervous system to help the body recover from the activation of the sympathetic system.

Most relaxation-based techniques ask a person to focus on a specific thought, word, image, or phrase. By focusing on just one item and giving it complete attention, the person is not thinking about all the things that are stressful. Together with the focus on a single object comes a slowing down of the breathing and the lowering of heart rate, respiration, circulation, and essentially all the functions of the body supervised by the parasympathetic nervous system. Most importantly, the different stress chemicals (catecholamines and cortisol) are no longer released. Most practices such as mindfulness, meditation, and yoga use this slowing down of the breath and the clearing of the thoughts to bring about stress relief. Mindfulness, in particular, involves intentionally bringing one's attention to the internal and external experiences occurring in the present moment and is often taught through a variety of meditation exercises. Mindfulness is a good practice to get used to as it has been empirically demonstrated to result in a number of positive health outcomes such as increased immune activity, less stress, and a host of other positive health outcomes.

You can try the guided imagery instructions in Table 1.3 and see how you feel.

Part 1.6 Best bet for health? Increase healthy behaviors

Coping with stress is perhaps one of the most important #psychhacks to be aware off. That said, to be healthy, you also need to practice many healthy behaviors and stay away from unhealthy ones. Easy to say of course but much harder to pull off, even as important as it is. How important can this be? Consider this: If everyone in North America stopped smoking today, the death rates due to cancer would drop by close to 30%.[20] If more North Americans ate better, got more physical activity, and cut down on their alcohol consumption, death rates would drop even further.

Healthy behaviors are defined as any specific actions that maintain and enhance health. These can range from the mundane (e.g., taking vitamins) to the critical (e.g., not smoking or not texting while driving). Many of our daily behaviors can influence our health and how long and how happily we live. Health psychologists use social psychological theories to explain why we perform healthy behaviors (and why we do not) and also to design and implement interventions to increase healthy behaviors.

An **intervention** can be defined as any program or message providing information or structure to change a behavior. If psychologists design a billboard to get people to stop smoking, for example, the billboard is considered an intervention. The outcome (change in smoking) can be assessed to

Table 1.3 Guided imagery instructions

Have a friend read these out to you slowly. Find a comfortable position and listen to the words and try to picture what is being said.

Picture yourself right now in a log cabin somewhere high up in the mountains.... It's wintertime, but even though it is very cold outside, you can enjoy the comfort of being in that cabin ... for inside of the cabin is a large fireplace with a brightly blazing fire providing plenty of heat and warmth ... and now you can go up to one of the windows and notice the frost on the windowpane ... you can even put your warm hand on the cold, hard glass of the windowpane feeling the heat from your hand and fingers melting the frost ... And then to get a view of the outside, you can begin to open the window, feeling it give way against the pressure of your hand; as the window opens, you take a big breath of that pure, fresh, cool mountain air and feel so good. Looking outside you can see the snow on the ground and lots of tall evergreen trees. And then looking off in the distance and seeing a wonderful view ... perhaps of a valley down below or other mountain peaks far, far in the distance.... . And now you can close the window and walk over to the fire feeling its warmth as you get closer.... . Go ahead and sit back in a comfortable chair facing the fire ... or if you wish, you can lie down next to the fire on a soft bearskin rug ... feeling the soothing warmth of the fire against your skin ... letting your body absorb the warmth bringing deep relaxation and comfort. ... You can also enjoy looking at the fire, seeing the burning logs, hearing the crackling of the logs and hissing sound from the sap encountering the fire ... smelling the fragrant smoke from the burning logs. You can even look around noticing the room as it is illuminated by the light from the fire ... noticing the flickering shadows on the walls ... noticing the furniture and any other objects in the room ... just look around and take it all in ... all the sights and sounds and smells ... feeling so peaceful in this place ... . so calm and completely tranquil. And you can be reminded that even though the cold wind is howling outside, you can feel so warm and comfortable inside ... letting that comfort spread to all parts of your mind. And in this place you have absolutely nothing to worry about ... for all that really matters is that you just allow yourself to enjoy the peacefulness, enjoy the deep comfort of being in this place right now ... as a relaxed, drowsy feeling comes over you ... and all the sights and sounds and smells gradually fade far away ... while you drift ... and float and dream in that cabin far off in the mountains. (Pause) And now, whenever you are ready, you can bring yourself back to a normal, alert, and wide-awake state by counting slowly from 1 to 3, so that when you reach the number 3 you will open your eyes feeling completely refreshed and comfortable.

determine whether the intervention was successful. The design and success of interventions often rely on one of the key themes of this book, "putting people first." When people want to stop smoking, drink less, or exercise more, they often turn to others for help. Most interventions make people turn to others for information or assistance.

Most common health problems are worsened, and in some cases even caused, by unhealthy behaviors.[1] For example, eating a lot of fatty foods and not getting enough physical exercise increase the likelihood of getting Type II diabetes and coronary heart disease. It is estimated that 50% of all deaths in the United States could have been postponed or avoided by changing unhealthy behaviors. Behavioral factors such as tobacco use, poor diet and activity patterns, and avoidable injuries are among the most prominent contributors to mortality.[21]

Health psychologists use a **biopsychosocial approach** to health, acknowledging that our health has biological, psychological, and social determinants. The *social* part of the term *biopsychosocial* is particularly important to social psychologists. For example, the media we are exposed to have a strong impact on the types of health behaviors we perform. The culture we live in and what we are surrounded by give us a lot of information about what is acceptable and what is not. As an example, consider movie watching.[22] Researchers[23] first counted the instances of smoking in each of 600 popular movies. They then gave teens a list of 50 recent popular films, selected randomly from this pool of 600 films. On the basis of the films each participant reported having seen, the researchers tallied the total number of times each teen would have been exposed to smoking or other tobacco use. More than 31% of teenagers who had seen 150 or more instances of actors smoking on film had tried smoking themselves, as compared to about 5% of teens who had seen 50 or fewer tobacco-related scenes. The number of teens who tried smoking increased with higher categories of exposure: 16% among students who viewed 0–50 movie tobacco occurrences; 21% among students who viewed 51–100 occurrences; 28% among students who viewed 101–150 occurrences; and 36% among students who viewed more than 150 occurrences. The association remained statistically significant after controlling for gender, grade in school, school performance, school, friend, sibling and parent smoking, sensation seeking, rebelliousness, and self-esteem.[24]

Celebrities have a lot more power than they may realize. In another recent study related to a newer tobacco habit, e-cigarettes, researchers looked at Instagram advertisements.[25] What if an ad has a celebrity endorsing a product as compared to a noncelebrity or if the ad just features the product itself? Participants who saw the celebrity endorsements had higher positive attitudes toward e-cigarettes and higher intensions to smoke. Not surprisingly, participants found the celebrities more trustworthy, attractive, and having more expertise than noncelebrities.

Social psychology also provides a mechanism for why movies are so important. Identifying with the movie characters is the problem. Men in one study watched movie clips with the male lead actor either smoking or not smoking.[26] The more the viewers identified with the actors, the greater the implicit associations between the self and smoking and the more the intention to smoke increased. The stronger associations uniquely predicted increases in smokers' intentions to smoke, over and above the effects of the viewer's explicit beliefs about smoking. This researcher establishes that exposure to smoking in movies is causally related to changes in smoking-related thoughts and that identifying with the actors is the key mechanism. Similar relationships between movie viewing and drinking have also been found.[27,28]

There are a lot of scientific reasons underlying behind whether to perform healthy behaviors or not. Next stop, a look at some of the theoretical approaches to changing health behaviors.

Part 1.7 Why don't we all just do it?

Given the importance of healthy behaviors, you may wonder why we all just do not do them more often. After all, the consequences of not doing them are clear. Too many unhealthy behaviors and you die earlier. Just like stress, psychological science has figured out many reasons why we do not do the behaviors we should. By getting a sense of the major theoretical reasons for poor behaviors you pave the path to developing your own #psychhacks to increasing your health behaviors.

In thinking about the challenges of behavior change, it might be valuable to take a moment here and check in on your own healthy behaviors. In Table 1.4 the Healthy Life Checklist is presented, and the researchers[29] offer this note about interpretation (p. 45):

> The first ten items are likely to increase your health and longevity. The next ten items are not only likely to help your health and longevity, but they also will make those extra years a lot more fun! Indeed, whereas a few of the first ten healthy lifestyle items sound like hard work, the last ten healthy lifestyle items make life more enjoyable.

The most commonly used theory in health psychology to explain health behavior activity is the **health belief model (HBM)**. The HBM represents one of the first theoretical approaches to studying the reasons people engage in healthy and unhealthy behaviors. According to the model, our beliefs

Table 1.4 Healthy life checklist

Select the items below that are true to you.
_____ 1. I don't smoke.
_____ 2. I never drink alcohol, or drink only moderately.
_____ 3. I am a normal weight (not too thin or obese).
_____ 4. I never talk on a cell phone while driving.
_____ 5. I use sunscreen whenever I am outdoors.
_____ 6. I eat fruits, vegetables, and a bit of dark chocolate every day.
_____ 7. I take a baby aspirin many days.
_____ 8. I exercise four or more times a week.
_____ 9. I regularly brush and floss my teeth.
_____ 10. I always wear seat belts.
_____ 11. I frequently feel happy and contented.
_____ 12. I engage in many activities that bring me joy.
_____ 13. I am satisfied with my life.
_____ 14. I feel sad only occasionally.
_____ 15. I feel angry only occasionally.
_____ 16. I feel stressed only occasionally.
_____ 17. I often feel grateful and generally trusting.
_____ 18. I have friends and family members on whom I can depend.
_____ 19. I am an optimistic person.
_____ 20. I am happy with my social relationships.

concerning the effectiveness, ease, and consequences of doing (or not doing) a certain behavior will determine whether we do (or do not do) that behavior. It is one of the most widely used frameworks and has been used for both behavior change and maintenance. It all began when a group of social psychologists were brought together at the U.S. Public Health Service to try and explain why people did not participate in programs to prevent or detect disease.[30,31] The model was then extended to explain people's responses to illness symptoms[32] and then to explain what influences whether people follow their prescribed treatments.[33]

The formulation of the health belief model provides a nice illustration of how social, cognitive, and behaviorist views have influenced health psychology. For example, learning theorists such as Skinner[34] believed that we learned to do a certain behavior if it was followed by a positive outcome (a reinforcement). So if exercising made us feel healthy, we would be more likely to exercise. Cognitive theorists added a focus on the *value* of an outcome (e.g., health) and the *expectation* that a particular action (e.g., exercise) will achieve that outcome. The health belief model is a value-expectancy theory in which the values and expectations have been reformulated from abstract concepts into health-related behaviors and concepts. For example, in the 1950s, a large number of eligible adults did not get themselves screened for tuberculosis, although tuberculosis was a big health problem and the screenings were free. In one study involving more than 1,200 adults, researchers found that 82% of the people who believed they were susceptible, and who believed early detection worked, had at least one voluntary chest X-ray.[40] Only 21% of the people who had neither belief got an X-ray.

How does the model explain health behavior? The model suggests that individuals will perform healthy behaviors if they believe they are susceptible to the health issue, if they believe it will have severe consequences, if they believe that their behavior will be beneficial in reducing the severity or susceptibility, and if they believe that the anticipated benefits of the behavior outweigh its costs (or barriers). Another factor that has been added to the model is the concept of self-efficacy,[35] which you will encounter again in this book.

Another way to try to predict whether someone is going to do something is to ascertain whether that person *intends* to do something. Behavioral intentions play a major role in many models of health behavior change, including the theory of reasoned action,[36] the theory of planned behavior,[37] the protection motivation theory,[38] and the concept of self-efficacy.[39]

So what is an intention? In these theories, intention is defined as a person's subjective probability that he or she will perform the behavior in question.[46] It is essentially an estimate of the probability of your doing something. If you are asked if you want dessert at the start of a meal when you are hungry, the probability that you will say yes is higher than it will be after the meal when you are stuffed.

The **theory of planned behavior** assumes that people decide to behave a certain way on the basis of intentions that depend on their attitude toward the behavior and their perceptions of the social norms regarding the behavior. As in the health beliefs model, attitudes toward the behavior are based on what the person believes to be the consequences of the behavior and how important these consequences are (both costs and benefits). Will eating dessert make you put on weight? Perception of social norms is your assessment of what others think about the behavior. Do the people you know support eating sweet treats? If you believe that everyone around you thinks that eating dessert is an acceptable behavior, you are more likely to want to do it. Of course, you may not care what people around you think. Your motivation to comply with others' preference is also part of the perception of social norms. If you care about the people around you *and* they support dessert eating, you are more likely to eat dessert.

Transtheoretical model. You can only change if you are really ready to change. Using this basic idea, the **transtheoretical model**[40,41] of behavior change was developed to identify common themes across different intervention theories (hence "*transtheoretical*"). The researchers who created the model suggest that we progress through different stages as we think about, attempt to, and finally change any specific behavior.

This model depicts change as a process occurring through a series of six stages. If you know what stage a person is in, you can tailor your intervention to fit the state of mind that the stage describes. People who are unaware that they are practicing a behavior that is unhealthy or do not intend to take any action to change a behavior (at least not in the next six months) are said to be in the precontemplation stage. People may have tried to change before, failed, and become demoralized, or they may just be misinformed about the actual consequences of their behavior. Some teenage smokers are so confident about their own health that they do not believe smoking is a problem for them and have no intention of changing. People in this stage avoid reading, thinking, or talking about their unhealthy behaviors. Health promotion programs are often wasted on them because they either do not know they have a problem or do not really care.

Part 1.8 Fighting sickness

Coping well with stress, increasing your healthy behaviors and decreasing your unhealthy behaviors can keep you healthy for some time. If we lived in a virus and bacteria–filled world or if we understood the nuances and biological bases of how illnesses develop you could bank on a long life. That is not the world we live in. Even healthy women and men fall sick and as witnessed by the COVID-19 pandemic, even all our science and vaccinations and health behaviors still have not kept thousands of people from dying. Sometimes sickness is a result of a genetic predisposition or not getting vaccinated. Sometimes it is shaking hands with the wrong person or not wearing a mask. Yes, that person who blew his running nose and did not wash. A major part of staying alive is doing the right thing when you feel the first symptoms of sickness or when full blown illness or disease descends.

With physical problems, it is often clear when you need to see a doctor. If your stomach hurts or if you develop a pain where there was no pain before, you will probably not let it be. Funnily enough, many psychological factors may influence how you recognize symptoms.

The confirmation bias. Once we believe something is true, we often change the way we interpret new information and the way we look at the world. We tend to try to confirm our belief, which biases how we process information. We have a **confirmation bias**. Psychologists have shown that if there is any ambiguity in a person's behavior, people are likely to interpret what they see in a way that is consistent with their bias.[42] If we believe that a change in our bodies is not a symptom of illness, we will probably look for information to support that belief. For example, if you are fair skinned and have spent too much time in the sun, there is a chance that you may develop some form of skin cancer.[43] The first signs are often round discolorations of the skin. You could look at one of these developing spots and believe that it is a blemish or a pimple, or that it was always there. Now when you look at your skin, you may try to draw attention to parts that look great, ignoring the developing skin spots. You confirm your bias that you are fine and cancer free by thinking that you have often had those spots, off and on, and they never meant anything before. You may even think that you have been feeling especially great recently, so it could not be the beginning of a problem.

This confirmation bias can lead to misperceptions of the social world and an accentuation of symptoms that do get attention. If you believe that you do not need to go to a doctor to seek treatment for flu-like symptoms or a cold, if you have managed to succeed on past occasions, or if you see others who do not seem to go in when they have symptoms, you may begin to overestimate how successful you can be by not going to a doctor. We not only find confirmation for what we expect to see, but we also tend to overestimate how often we are right.[44] This is the *illusory correlation*, in which you believe your expectation has been correct more times than it actually has been. Confirmation biases occur partly because we ignore disconfirmations of our biases and selectively remember information that supports our biases.[45]

Attributions and misattributions. Another psychological process that can influence the recognition of symptoms is related to how we determine the cause of events. The cognitive process of assigning meaning to a symptom or behavior is referred to as making **attributions**.[46] Many factors influence our attributions.[47] If your stomach hurts, you may attribute it to what you just ate. If you have not eaten anything different recently, you are more likely to worry about a stomach pain than if you have just tried something that is very different (spicier or oilier than you are used to). How you attribute a pain in your chest may depend on physical factors, such as your age, or psychological factors, such as beliefs that you hold about illness in general. A teenager may think of a chest pain as gas or a cramp; an older person may worry about a heart attack. The cause you attribute your symptoms to can influence whether or not you seek treatment.

Sometimes we mistakenly label our physiological experiences based on external factors.[48] If you feel tired and a lot of people you work with have colds, you are likely to attribute your tiredness to your developing a cold, even though it could be due to your not getting enough sleep. This misattribution can increase your anxiety, and in combination with a confirmation bias (that you have a cold), you may soon find yourself accumulating more evidence to support your theory. Your belief that you are getting sick will, in essence, make you sick (a self-fulfilling prophecy).

Other specific individual differences influence how patients fare in the health care process. Patients vary in how much they want to be involved in their treatment and how much information they want. **Behavioral involvement** includes the patient's attitude toward self-care, specifically an active involvement in treatment. **Informational involvement** measures how much the patient wants to know about his or her illness and specific details of its treatment. In a study of male coronary bypass patients, patients who had a high compared with a low desire for behavioral involvement experienced less ambulation dysfunction, fewer social interaction problems, and less emotional upset immediately after release from the hospital. Patients who had a high compared with a low desire for information involvement experienced more social interaction and emotional problems during this period.

Once you recognize you have a problem, you have to decide to seek treatment. People sometimes take a lot of time to recognize they have symptoms; this is **appraisal delay**, and many psychological factors discussed previously can prevent symptom recognition. Appraisal delay can lead to **illness delay**, the time between the recognition that one is ill to the decision to seek care. Finally, there are often **utilization delays** between the decision to seek care and the actual behaviors to obtain medical health care. The big #psychhack here. **Recognize** these natural tendencies we have to delay and **avoid** them!

There is one more thought to bear in mind with sickness. If you go in to the doctor and are prescribed treatment, whether medication or behavior, it is a good idea to follow the doctor's orders. The extent to which a patient's behavior matches with his or her practitioner's advice is referred to as **adherence** and a major reason for not getting well quickly is nonadherence. If you are someone who has not completed a course of antibiotics, you will not be surprised to hear that many patients do not take all their medications. There are many practical concerns that influence adherence. As you can guess, adherence rates vary according to the type of treatment prescribed and to the disease or illness you have. As you can see, many different steps are involved in the process of getting sick and recovering.

Part 1.9 Putting it all together: Your physical health

Understanding why we do or do not do something is important because it provides us with a way to change and make a difference in our health. Armed with knowledge about the determinants of health behaviors and the methodological rigor of psychology, researchers attempt to intervene to change behaviors. Psychologists have tried different techniques to get people to do what is healthy by designing interventions based on the theories discussed previously and using the scientific method to bring about change. Different interventions focus on different antecedents of behavior. Some psychologists seek to change people's attitudes to change their behavior; others attempt to change their beliefs or intentions. The way an intervention is designed can depend on the specific behavior that needs to be changed, the funding available for the behavior change, and the number of people that the intervention has to reach.

As you can see, psychological theories can be applied to understanding many different aspects of health, ranging from why we get stressed and how we cope with it to modifying our health behaviors and predicting how we recognize symptoms and report them. Applying a psychological perspective to the study of health illustrates the benefits of considering people as active constructors of their own realities, with health behaviors depending on the interaction of the person and the situation. You may find these insights useful in optimizing your own health.

Notes

1 Jakicic, J. M., Davis, K. K., Rogers, R. J., King, W. C., Marcus, M. D., Helsel, D., … Belle, S. H. (2016). Effect of wearing technology combined with a lifestyle intervention on long-term weight loss: The IDEA randomized clinical trial. *Journal of the American Medical Association, 316*(11), 1161–1171. https://doi.org/10.1001/jama.2016.12858

2 World Health Organization (2003). *WHO definition of health*. Preamble to the Constitution of the World Health Organization as adopted by the International Health Conference, New York, 19–22 June 1946; signed on 22 July 1946 by the representatives of 61 states (Official Records of the World Health Organization, no. 2, p. 100) and entered into force on 7 April 1948. www.who.int/about/definition/en/print.html

3 Gurung, R. A. R. (2014). *Health psychology: A cultural approach* (3rd ed.). Cengage.

4 Cannon, W. B. (1929). *Bodily changes in pain, hunger, fear and rage*. Oxford.

5 Seyle, H. (1956). *The stress of life*. McGraw-Hill.

6 Cannon, W. B. (1914). The interrelations of emotions as suggested by recent physiological researches. *American Journal of Physiology, 25*(2), 256–282.

7 Eiland, L., & McEwen, B. S. (2012). Early life stress followed by subsequent adult chronic stress potentiates anxiety and blunts hippocampal structural remodeling. *Hippocampus, 22*(1), 82–91. https://doi.org/10.1002/hipo.20862

8 McEwen, B., & Lasley, E. (2007). Allostatic load: When protection gives way to damage. In A. Monat, R. S. Lazarus, G. Reevy, A. Monat, R. S. Lazarus, & G. Reevy (Eds.), *The Praeger handbook on stress and coping* (Vol. 1, pp. 99–109). Praeger/Greenwood.

9 Lazarus, R. S. (1966). *Psychological stress and the coping process*. McGraw-Hill.

10 Lazarus, R. S. (1991). Progress on a cognitive-motivational-relational theory of emotion. *American Psychologist, 46*(8), 819–834.

11 Langer, E. J., & Rodin, J. (1976). The effects of choice and enhanced personal responsibility for the aged: A field experiment in an institutional setting. *Journal of Personality and Social Psychology, 34*(2), 191–198.

12 Taylor, S. E., Klein, L. C., Lewis, B. P., Gruenewald, T. L., Gurung, R. A. R., & Udpegraff, J. A. (2000). Biobehavioral responses to stress in females: Tend-and-befriend, not fight-or-flight. *Psychological Review, 107*(3), 411–429.

13 Taylor, S. E., & Master, S. L. (2011). Social responses to stress: The tend-and-befriend model. In R. J. Contrada, A. Baum, R. J. Contrada, & A. Baum (Eds.), *The handbook of stress science: Biology, psychology, and health* (pp. 101–109). Springer.

14 Repetti, R. L. (1997). *The effects of daily job stress on parent behavior with preadolescents.* Paper presented at the biennial meeting of the Society for Research in Child Development, Washington, DC.

15 Barsky, A. J. (1988). *Worried sick: Our troubled quest for wellness.* Little Brown and Co.

16 Holder-Perkins, V., & Wise, T. N. (2001). Somatization disorder. In K. A. Phillips (Ed.), *Somatoform and factitious disorders* (pp. 1–26). American Psychiatric Association.

17 McWilliams, L. A., Cox, B. J., & Enns, M. W. (2003). Mood and anxiety disorders associated with chronic pain: An examination in a nationally representative sample. *Pain, 106*(1–2), 127–133. https://doi.org/10.1016/S0304-3959(03)00301-4.

18 Pearlin, L. I., & Schooler, C. (1978). The structure of coping. *Journal of Health and Social Behavior, 19*(1), 2–21. https://doi.org/10.2307/2136319

19 Folkman, S., & Lazarus, R. S. (1988). Coping as a mediator of emotion. *Journal of Personality and Social Psychology, 54*(3), 466–475. https://doi.org/10.1037/0022-3514.54.3.466

20 Gurung, R. A. R. (2019). *Health psychology:Well-being in a diverse world.* (4th ed.). Sage.

21 Centers for Disease Control and Prevention. (2012). *Vital signs.* www.cdc.gov/tobacco/data_statistics/vital_signs/index.htm

22 Wills, T., Sargent, J., Stoolmiller, M., Gibbons, F., & Gerrard, M. (2008). Movie smoking exposure and smoking onset: A longitudinal study of mediation processes in a representative sample of U.S. adolescents. *Psychology of Addictive Behaviors, 22*(2), 269–277.

23 Sargent, J. D., Dalton, M. A., Heatherton, T., & Beach, M. (2003). Modifying exposure to smoking depicted in movies: A novel approach to preventing adolescent smoking. *Archives of Pediatrics and Adolescent Medicine, 157*(7), 643–648.

24 Sargent, J. D., Dalton, M. A., Beach, M. L., Mott, L. A., Tickle, J. J., Ahrens, M. B., & Heatherton, T. (2002). Viewing tobacco use in movies: Does it shape attitudes that mediate adolescent smoking? *American Journal of Preventive Medicine, 22*(3), 137–145.

25 Phua, J., Jin, S. V., & Ham, J. M. (2018). Celebrity-endorsed e-cigarette brand Instagram advertisements: Effects on young adults' attitudes towards e-cigarettes and smoking intensions. *Journal of Health Psychology, 23*(4), 550–560. doi.org/10.1177/1359105317693912

26 Dal Cin, S., Gibson, B., Zanna, M., Shumate, R., & Fong, G. (2007). Smoking in movies, implicit associations of smoking with the self, and intentions to smoke. *Psychological Science, 18*(7), 559–563.

27 Dal Cin, S., Worth, K., Dalton, M., & Sargent, J. (2008). Youth exposure to alcohol use and brand appearances in popular contemporary movies. *Addiction, 103*(12), 1925–1932.

28 Dalton, M. A., Ahrens, M. B., Sargent, J. D., Mott, L. A., Beach, M. L., Tickle, J. J., & Heatherton, T. (2002). Relation between parental restrictions on movies and adolescent use of tobacco and alcohol. *Effective Clinical Practice, 5*(1), 1–10.

29 Diener, E., & Biswas-Diener, R. (2008). *Happiness: Unlocking the mysteries of psychological wealth*. Blackwell Publishing.

30 Hochbaum, G. M. (1958). *Public participation in medical screening programs: A sociopsychological study*. PHS publication no. 572. Washington, DC: Government Printing Office. Holder-Perkins & Wise.

31 Rosenstock, I. M. (1960). What research in motivation suggests for public health. *American Journal of Public Health, 50*(3), 295–301.

32 Kirscht, J. P. (1971). Social and psychological problems of surveys on health and illness. *Social Science and Medicine, 5*(6), 519–526.

33 Becker, M. H. (Ed.). (1974). *The health belief model and personal health behavior*. Slack Press.

34 Skinner, B. F. (1938). *The behavior of organisms*. Appleton-Century-Crofts.

35 Rosenstock, I. M., Strecher, V. J., & Becker, M. H. (1988). The health belief model and HIV risk behavior change. In J. Peterson & R. DiClemente (Eds.), *Preventing AIDS: Theory and practice of behavior interventions* (pp. 5–24). Plenum Press.

36 Fishbein, M., & Ajzen, I. (1975). *Belief, attitude, intention and behavior: An introduction to theory and research*. Addison-Wesley.

37 Ajzen, I. (1988). *Attitudes, personality, and behavior*. Dorsey Press.

38 Rogers, E. M. (1983). *Diffusion of innovations*. Free Press.

39 Bandura, A. (1977). *Social learning theory*. Prentice Hall.

40 Prochaska, J. O., Wright, J. A., & Velicer, W. F. (2008). Evaluating theories of health behavior change: A hierarchy of criteria applied to the transtheoretical model. *Applied Psychology: An International Review, 57*(4), 561–588. https://doi.org/10.1111/j.1464-0597.2008.00345.x

41 Prochaska, J. O., & Prochaska, J. M. (2010). Self-directed change: A transtheoretical model. In J. E. Maddux & J. P. Tangney (Eds.), *Social psychological foundations of clinical psychology* (pp. 431–440). Guilford Press.

42 Olson, J. M., Roese, N. J., & Zanna, M. P. (1996). Expectancies. In E. T. Higgins & A. W. Kruglanski (Eds.), *Social psychology: Handbook of basic principles* (pp. 211–239). Guilford Press.

43 Stack, S. (2003). Media coverage as a risk factor in suicide. *Journal of Epidemiology and Community Health, 57*(4), 238–240.

44 Shavitt, S., Sanbonmatsu, D. M., Smittipatana, S., & Posavac, S. S. (1999). Broadening the conditions for illusory correlation formation: Implications for judging minority groups. *Basic and Applied Social Psychology, 21*(4), 263–279.

45 Fiske, S. T. (2004). *Social beings: A core motives approach to social psychology*. Wiley.

46 Jones, E. E., Kannouse, D. E., Kelley, H. H., Nisbett, R. E., Valins, S., & Weiner, B. (Eds.). (1972). *Attribution: Perceiving the causes of behavior*. General Learning Press.

47 Miller, S. M., & Diefenbach, M. A. (1998). The Cognitive-Social Health Information-Processing (C-SHIP) model: A theoretical framework for research in behavioral oncology. In D. S. Krantz & A. Baum (Eds.), *Technology and methods in behavioral medicine* (pp. 219–244). Lawrence Erlbaum.

48 Schachter, S., & Singer, J. E. (1962). Cognitive, social, and physiological determinants of emotional state. *Psychological Review, 69*, 379–399.

Section 2 My mental health

Part 2.1 Normal, abnormal, and why these are not good word choices

Reverend Howard Finster was a bicycle repairman and preacher who, according to folklore, retired from preaching when he realized that no one could remember his sermons. While painting a bicycle, Finster had his first vision – a face emerged from the bicycle paint on the end of his finger while a voice instructed him to create sacred art.[1,2,3]

Finster was not trained as an artist, but he began creating art anyway and turned his property into a museum of sorts. He called it Paradise Gardens, and filled it over the decades with tens of thousands of pieces of art: Quirky sculptures often made of other people's trash, vibrant paintings incorporating biblical verses and pop culture, and whimsical buildings that were often quite crooked because he did not use standard tools, such as a level. After his death in 2001, Paradise Gardens quickly fell into disrepair.[4] But in recent years, admirers of Finster have raised money and begun the process of restoring his life's work.[5]

Sometimes, a creative genius like Finster gets labeled with stigmatizing words: Strange, crazy, kooky, eccentric, weird, and even "abnormal." But what does it mean to be "abnormal"? Why is the word "abnormal" problematic? And how should we think about mental illness?

Defining what exactly we mean by the words "normal" and "abnormal" is among the most vexing questions faced by mental health clinicians, and there is no clear consensus. In fact, many agree that we shouldn't use those words at all because of their stigmatizing nature! Most clinicians agree that a **mental illness** includes one or more of the following criteria, sometimes called "the four Ds": deviation, distress, dysfunction, and danger.[6,7]

Deviation. Deviation refers to behaviors that deviate, or vary, from a **norm**, a guideline for an appropriate attitude or behavior. As one example, it is a norm in our society to eat enough to maintain a body weight that can sustain our organs. Some people, often young women in Western countries, engage in behaviors such as dieting and excessive exercise with the intention of losing an unhealthy amount of weight. This deviation from eating-related norms is an indication that this behavior may be abnormal.

DOI: 10.4324/9781003188711-3

There are two problems with the concept of deviation as a marker for abnormality. First, norms are often subjective, and are rooted in a certain time and place that is represented by our culture. Second, deviation is not always a bad thing. Think about Howard Finster. He certainly deviated from the norms for his culture, but would you label him "abnormal" or simply unusual? He apparently enjoyed his life as an artist and became famous – his work is now held in many museums, including the Smithsonian Museum in the United States.

Distress. A second criterion for abnormal behavior is the experience of distress in conjunction with that behavior. For example, a person experiencing symptoms of depression is often quite upset or distressed by these symptoms. A depressed person, therefore, would meet both the criteria of deviation and distress. Howard Finster, by most accounts, was not distressed by his behavior, even though his behavior deviated from norms.

Dangerousness. A third criterion for abnormal/atypical behavior is that it is dangerous, whether to the person engaged in that behavior or to others around him or her. For example, anorexia nervosa, a common eating disorder, is among the most fatal of all mental illnesses.[8]

However, many behaviors that are classified as being part of a mental illness are not dangerous. Anxiety and mood disorders together make up the bulk of mental health diagnoses; yet, except when suicidal thoughts are present, these disorders are not likely to cause immediate physical harm. Moreover, many behaviors do not necessarily represent abnormality from a mental health perspective, but are clearly dangerous, such as getting in a car driven by your drunk friend. Many extreme sports, from ice climbing to deep-sea scuba diving, also carry known risks, yet don't represent mental illness.

Dysfunction. The final of the four Ds is dysfunction. Dysfunctional behavior is maladaptive; it interferes with our ability to participate fully in society. Maladaptive behavior might refer to problems appropriately grooming ourselves, holding down a job, or maintaining interpersonal relationships. Most behaviors that we consider "abnormal" from a mental health perspective are dysfunctional, even if they are not dangerous or causing distress. Depressed people might isolate themselves, and anxious people might avoid taking a particular job out of fear.

The bottom line, according to the four D model, is that a psychological disorder is a cluster of symptoms that represents deviance (is atypical) and is dysfunctional. It also may be dangerous and is almost always distressing.

How do psychological disorders impact individuals and communities? Mental illness is quite common. A global survey of approximately 85,000 people from countries around the world found a lifetime prevalence rate of about one-third, with a rate of about 50% among people in the United States.[9,10] These numbers have spiked since the COVID-19 pandemic, particularly for anxiety and depressive disorders.[11,12] One compilation of studies found that about half of the world's population experienced psychological distress related to anxiety, depression, or sleep problems with rates even higher among COVID-19 patients and healthcare workers.[13]

Part 2.2 The difficulty of diagnosing mental illness

In the United States, currently, diagnoses of mental illness are compiled in a thick book published by the American Psychiatric Association with input from hundreds of professionals around the world. It's called the DSM-5, short for the *Diagnostic and Statistical Manual of Mental Disorders*, Fifth Edition, and it includes over 260 different diagnoses.[14]

Globally, the World Health Organization (WHO) publishes the *International Classification of Diseases* (ICD),[15] and the DSM-5 provides ICD codes alongside the DSM codes for every disorder. In general, the DSM and the ICD are used similarly, and have similar benefits and drawbacks.

What are the benefits?[16] A standard diagnostic system offers a simple method for professionals to communicate with one another. So, a health insurance company can quickly get the information necessary to authorize treatment, and a psychiatrist to whom a patient has been referred by a psychologist can understand a lot from the existing diagnostic codes. It also helps clinicians to determine a treatment plan because research on psychological disorders is based on the codes in the DSM.

Sounds great, right? Not completely. One of the most important criticisms is that DSM diagnoses are categorical.[17] That is, you either have a disorder or you don't. But we all know that it is indeed possible to be a little bit anxious. Knowing that someone does – or does not – meet the criteria for an anxiety disorder doesn't tell us much about their overall level of anxiety.

Another criticism involves the ever-expanding roster of diagnoses. DSM-5 has more diagnoses than in the past, a situation that some critics have called "reckless hyperinflation."[18] Some critics assert that these expansions are due to so many contributors championing the disorder of their expertise, whereas other critics cite financial conflicts of interest – connections to the pharmaceutical industry, for example.[19]

We, the general public, might not be as likely to benefit from an expansion of what qualifies as a psychological disorder. There are very real consequences that occur when we receive the label of a mental illness. One study found that the following were the terms that most easily came to mind among the general public: Nuts, psycho, crazy, loony, weird, freak, and screw loose.[20] This stigma extends to treatment, leading many of us to imagine an "insane asylum" out of a horror film rather than the reality, which is usually a modern hospital or outpatient setting.

It's clear that there's a stigma associated with psychological disorders, and that stigma is often associated with prejudice and discrimination. We hope that you, by learning more about psychological disorders, and by reading some real-life examples, will experience less stigma toward people with psychological disorders – including yourself, given that many of you and your loved ones will experience, or have experienced, a psychological disorder at some point in your lives.

However, the normalization of negative reactions to many situations can have positive consequences – that is, it's quite typical to be sad in the face of a loss or anxious after experiencing, for example, a natural disaster.[21,22] In fact, research suggests that most people exposed to a major trauma are resilient.[23] (Later in this section, we'll explore how the research on resilience can help us in our own lives.)

A final note about DSM-5. In acknowledgement of the importance of social and cultural aspects of psychological disorders, the DSM-5 includes much more information about culture than previous editions. For each disorder, there is a section called "culture-related diagnostic issues" for each disorder that outlines ways in which that disorder may vary based on a person's culture, race, ethnicity, or home country. For example, the DSM-5 explains that the specific situations that people with panic disorder fear can be culturally driven – the wind as a trigger, for example, in Vietnam. These important additions to the DSM remind us that our own cultural experiences and beliefs can affect whether and how we exhibit psychological distress.

In summary, despite the DSM-5's flaws, along with the general flaws of labeling people with a mental illness, the DSM-5 remains the go-to method of diagnosing mental illness in the United States (and the ICD plays that role in much of the rest of the world).[24]

Part 2.3 Why not just snap out of a depressed mood?

Depression. Tennis star Naomi Osaka withdrew from the 2021 French Open after just one match rather than participate in the post-match news conferences that she saw as mentally draining.[25] As explanation, Osaka described struggling with "long bouts of depression" over the preceding several years. She may have been suffering from the most common mood disorder, **major depressive disorder** (MDD). Someone suffering from MDD experiences change in emotions, cognitions, and physical qualities and behaviors. It's much more than the temporary bad mood that every one of us experiences from time to time.

What are the symptoms of depression? Before we consider depression further, we suggest that you go online and search for a brief assessment called the Zung Self-Rating Depression Scale.[26] There's one version, with scoring information at the bottom, here: wia.unl.edu/documents/2017/zung-self-rating-depression-scale.pdf. (It's an old scale, but recent researchers suggest it still holds up.[27]) [A brief note: For any of the scales in this section, if you are concerned about your score, go straight to the section on how to find a clinician. Many people respond well to psychological and psychiatric treatment, and it's just as important not to neglect your mental health as it is not to neglect your physical health.]

If you took the Zung scale, you will have seen the range of symptoms. Emotional symptoms include hopelessness and sadness; cognitive symptoms include negative thoughts or difficulty concentrating or making decisions; and physical qualities or behaviors include difficulty sleeping or a lack of motivation to do things. Osaka's description of her experience with depression hints at these types of symptoms, and her willingness to talk about her struggles put a face to a disorder that so many people experience.

How common is depression? Depression is incredibly common, to the degree that it is sometimes called the common cold of psychological disorders. One large-scale United States survey study found that more than 20% of people will experience some kind of a mood disorder at some point in their lives.[28] Globally, almost 5% of people suffer from major depressive disorder at any given time,[29] a rate that is more like 7% among people in the United States.[30] And from adolescence through adulthood, women are twice as likely to experience depression as men.[31]

What are some of the causes of depression? For any psychological disorder, researchers and clinicians tend to use what they call the "developmental psychopathology model" to understand its causes. This means, basically, that a range of factors across someone's development as a person interact to make them vulnerable (or not) to suffering from a mental illness.[32] These include biological factors, psychological factors, and social and cultural factors. For each disorder, we'll describe some of these factors, but it's important to remember that we won't list all factors. In fact, researchers likely haven't even discovered them all.

Let's look specifically at depression. First, there is a clear genetic component. Studies of twins have found that people are more likely to experience depression if they have an identical twin – with whom they share 100% of their genes – who has depression than if they have a fraternal twin – with whom they share 50% of their genes – with depression.[33] Moreover, researchers are starting to pinpoint the locations of genes that seem to increase the risk for depression.[34]

How might genes influence depression? There are theories that involve both differences in neurotransmitters, the chemical messengers that help the neurons in our brain and body communicate, and differences in brain structure, the parts of the brain. Too little or too much of a range of neurotransmitters – including serotonin, dopamine, and glutamate – has been linked with depression.[35] So have structural changes in parts of the brain.[36,37] The ways in which brain chemistry and structure drive depression are too complicated to discuss here – and not even fully understood by researchers – but it's important to be aware that depression has biological roots, which likely is part of why people with depression can't just "snap out of it."

But there are psychological risk factors, too. Both chronic stress, such as a long pandemic, and sudden stressful life events, such as experiences of racism or xenophobia, are related to depression.[38,39,40] In addition, stress seems to affect depressed people more than nondepressed people; one study found that people who suffer from depression exhibit poorer recovery – in terms of cortisol levels – than people who don't suffer from depression.[41]

Finally, there are social and cultural factors, both of which are almost certainly entwined with the biological and psychological factors we discussed previously. Earlier, we mentioned that women, across most of the lifespan, are twice as likely to suffer from depression as men. There also are differences based on race and ethnicity; for example, in the United States, people who are Black, Latino, or Native American experience higher rates of depression than people who are White, likely because of the higher average stress levels, including discrimination, experienced by many in these communities.[42] In addition, there are global differences. For example, prevalence rates are particularly high in Africa and South Asia, perhaps because of higher levels of chronic stress, including politically driven conflicts.[43]

What is the typical outcome? The typical major depressive episode lasts about four months,[44] and research suggests that as many as 85% of people who experience a major depressive episode will eventually experience another.[45,46] Moreover, the risk of another episode increases with every additional episode that a person experiences.[47] Additional bad news is that many people never seek treatment for depression. Globally, researchers estimate that about 56% of people with depression go untreated.[48] Moreover, researchers suggest that the median length of time until someone receives their first treatment is eight years.[49]

But it's not all bad news. Treatment – either with medications or psychotherapy – leads to improvement more quickly than would occur naturally, and it decreases the risk of a relapse.[50] And you'll learn more about antidepressants and psychotherapy for depression later in the section. Our advice? The same for all psychological disorders. If you think that you or a friend or family member is suffering from depression, turn to the treatment part of this section for advice on how to get help.

Part 2.4 Does feeling anxious = anxiety disorder?

Kara Baskin wrote about her Hawaii honeymoon on a *New York Times* blog.[51] She reported that she got winks from friends when she told them that she and her new husband never left their hotel; however, the reason was a painful one. Their self-imposed exile from honeymoon fun on the island of Maui was due solely to Kara's anxiety. For years, she had experienced **panic attacks**, episodes of intense fear that occur out of the blue, and that are accompanied by alarming physical sensations. Kara's fear of future panic attacks kept her caged in her room, a fear of open spaces called agoraphobia.

In her blog post, Kara tries to explain the severity of a panic attack. It's not, she tells us, the everyday anxiety of work or dating. It feels more like you're dying – like you're having a heart attack or you're drowning. She explains:

> Your heart pounds, your chest tightens, you sweat and gasp as dread sets in. It's like looking at the world from inside an aquarium: Everyone is moving so languidly, so infuriatingly unaware – while you're rattling around inside yourself on speed wondering where your next breath might come from, or if it will come at all.[52]

Before we consider panic disorder further, we suggest you do an online search for the brief (and free) measure called the Zung Self-Rating Anxiety Scale.[53] One online version is in this link: mentalhealthprofessionalsinc.com/Forms/Zung_Self-Rating_Anxiety_Scale.pdf. The scoring for the scale is at the end. (As with the Zung depression scale, the anxiety scale is old, but recent researchers believe that it also holds up.[54]) As with depression, **anxiety** has a range of symptoms – emotional symptoms like nervousness and fear, cognitive symptoms like thoughts that something bad will happen, physical symptoms like numbness and dizziness, and behavioral symptoms like avoidance. The Zung anxiety measure focuses on symptoms of anxiety more broadly, rather than just the symptoms of a panic attack. Someone with a very high score might have a psychological disorder called generalized anxiety disorder (GAD). Someone with GAD is an excessive worrier, to a degree that their ability to function in life is affected. Here, however, we're going to explore in more depth panic disorder, the psychological disorder you were introduced to at the beginning of this section. Let's start by considering the symptoms that would lead to a diagnosis of panic disorder. You'll see that many of the symptoms on the Zung scale occur with panic disorder, albeit in a much more extreme way than with GAD.

What are the symptoms of panic disorder? According to the DSM-5, panic disorder is diagnosed when someone has repeated panic attacks that occur seemingly out of the blue and worries frequently about having more panic attacks. They also might avoid situations in which an attack might occur. So, panic attacks are both dysfunctional and distressing. What's a panic attack? Per the DSM-5, someone must quickly – within minutes – spiral into a state of extreme fear that might involve symptoms such as heart palpitations, shortness of breath, feelings of choking, dizziness, a fear of having a heart attack or dying, and a fear of losing control.

You'll notice that, like depression and GAD, panic disorder involves emotion-related, cognitive, physical, and behavioral symptoms. Fear is an example of an emotional symptom, and the thoughts that drive that fear, such as a belief that one is dying, are cognitive symptoms. There are numerous physical symptoms, like heart palpitations, and behaviorally, people often avoid or flee situations that they view as triggering panic attacks. The blogger whom we met earlier, Kara Baskin, described having a panic attack in a Mexican restaurant. "Halfway through the meal, my heart fluttered. Then it fluttered again. Then I had a kind of out-of-body sensation, the notion of hovering above my cactus-leaf margarita."[55] This particular panic attack was so frightening that Kara went to the hospital, fearful of heart problems.

The physical symptoms are alarming if they are not tied to an obvious trigger, as in Kara's apparently out-of-the-blue symptoms at the Mexican restaurant. If you've never experienced a panic attack, you can experience some of the physical symptoms for yourself if you hyperventilate – breathing in and out rapidly – for 30–60 seconds. If you do this, notice any physical sensations, such as increased heart rate or tingling fingers. Of course, because you know what's causing the symptoms, they're likely not frightening. And you can quickly get rid of them by spending a few minutes focusing on slowing your breathing and relaxing your body. But imagine if these symptoms emerged seemingly for no reason. You were, say, sitting at your desk and started feeling this way. That would likely be frightening.

An ongoing fear of panic attacks can lead to agoraphobia, as it did in Kara's case. According to DSM-5, people with agoraphobia are afraid of, and avoid, situations such as public transportation, crowded stores, and open spaces like bridges. If avoidance of any of these places appears to ward off panic attacks, the tendency to want to avoid that place is rewarded and becomes stronger.

How common is panic disorder? Globally, anxiety disorders as a whole are second only to depressive disorders in their impact on people's lives.[56] They will affect almost 30% of people in the United States over the course of their lives.[57] And they are the most common psychological disorder in many countries around the world with rates ranging from about 5% to about 30%.[58] The most common anxiety disorders are the **phobias** – dysfunctional and irrational fears of, say, dogs or heights. More than 12% of Americans experience a phobia at some point in their lives. In the United States, panic disorder afflicts almost 5% of the population, and generalized anxiety disorder afflicts almost 6%.[59]

What are some of the causes of panic disorder? As with other psychological disorders, a **panic disorder** is driven by biological, psychological, and social and cultural factors, with likely interactions among these factors. First, there are biological aspects of panic disorder. For example, there is evidence that genetics are involved, in part because panic disorder tends to run in families.[60,61] But there are other biological aspects, too. As with other disorders, there also are links to specific brain structures and to several neurotransmitters, with a growing body of research that aims to understand these mechanisms.[62]

One of the main psychological risk factors for panic disorder is a cognitive symptom – a high level of what is called anxiety sensitivity.[63] Anxiety sensitivity occurs when someone is overly attuned to any physical sensations in their body, with a subsequent misinterpretation of those sensations as dangerous. So, if someone exercises, drinks caffeine, or has sex and then has an increased heart rate, that sensation might be interpreted as potentially harmful – a heart attack in the making, for example. If a panic attack results from this sensitivity, this may lead to worry about having future panic attacks, another risk factor for developing full-fledged panic disorder.[64] There also are social and cultural factors. Coinciding with the psychological risk factor of stress, panic disorder occurs more often among women than men, and is more common among those facing stressors that may be related to social structures or to culture, such as chronic economic hardship.[65,66]

What is the typical outcome? There is a high rate of success in the treatment of panic disorder. The gold standard is **cognitive-behavior therapy**, known as CBT for short, about which you'll learn more later.[67] Medications and CBT seem to work equally well in the treatment of panic disorder.[68] However, researchers suggests that CBT might be superior to medication because relapse rates are lower – that is, improvements are more likely to be lasting ones.[69] CBT teaches patients skills – cognitive skills that help them challenge their misinterpretations of bodily symptoms, and behavioral skills like relaxation and breathing techniques that help reduce anxiety – and then has patients expose themselves to panic symptoms to learn to manage them.[70,71]

The problem, as with the treatment for other disorders, is that many people do not seek out or fail to receive treatment.[72,73,74] Moreover, even among those who do receive treatment, there are a number of barriers that can limit its success, including a reluctance to do the "homework" that CBT requires between sessions and the presence of stressful or chaotic circumstances in patients' lives.[75] Our advice for those suffering from panic disorder? Seek treatment. Don't delay. And do your homework.

Part 2.5 Someone in my family may have an eating disorder. Can I help?

A person with anorexia nervosa is not simply thin. She – and it's usually a she – is unhealthily thin. Ask Katy Waldman. In an article about her and her twin sister's battles with anorexia, she wrote:

> I have nothing pretty to say about my body when I get too thin. My skin dulls and develops scaly patches; my oversized noggin bobs on my pencil-neck like an idiot balloon. Eating disorder memoirists love to fetishize hipbones, but I am here to tell you that mine made zero aesthetic contributions to my stomach area. My hair! Stringy, limp…[76]

Despite the fact that she could see that her own extreme weight loss did not lead to beauty or to a confident body image, Katy felt compelled to maintain an unhealthy thinness.

In her article, she explains her struggles to understand why she and her sister developed anorexia. Was it a perfectionistic personality? Were there genetic contributions? Did it derive from the part of their brains that regulates eating and hunger? With respect to herself, was her anorexia fueled by unhealthy competition and comparisons with her sister? Whatever its roots, Katy describes the sense of inevitability as her eating disorder intensified: "I had skipped meals and counted calories and performed crunches until the illness reached through the mirror and grabbed me and it was too late."[77]

Before we describe the symptoms of and research on **anorexia nervosa**, search online for the 26-item Eating Attitudes Test (EAT-26), a classic and freely available scale that measures disordered eating.[78] You can find a self-scoring version here: eat-26.com/eat-26. If you're concerned about your score, go to the part in this section on finding a clinician.

What are the symptoms of anorexia nervosa? According to the DSM-5, people are diagnosed with anorexia nervosa when they have an unhealthily low weight as a result of their behaviors, such as eating too little or burning too many calories through exercise. As you saw from the EAT-26, disordered eating includes not just a behavioral component, but also an emotional component, such as fear of being overweight, and a cognitive component, such as a person's belief that they must be perfect or must control their eating.

How common is anorexia nervosa? Anorexia nervosa occurs in an estimated less-than-1% of women, with far lower rates in men.[79,80] Researchers estimate that anywhere from three to ten times as many women, compared to men, suffer from eating disorders, including anorexia nervosa.[81,82] Among men who have an eating disorder, a disproportionate number of them are gay, bisexual, or transgender.[83] More than half of people with anorexia also suffer from another psychological disorders – often an anxiety disorder or a mood disorder.[84] Unlike the other disorders we've considered, there's not much research on the global prevalence of eating disorders, perhaps because there's debate about whether eating disorders are specific to certain cultures.

What are some of the causes of anorexia nervosa? As with other psychological disorders, a wide range of factors is involved in the development of anorexia nervosa. Researchers show that there are genetic risk factors for anorexia.[85] Moreover, we know that anorexia nervosa runs in families. In addition, if someone has an identical twin with anorexia, his or her chances of developing anorexia are higher than if he or she has a fraternal twin with anorexia nervosa.[86] There also is evidence that an imbalance of neurotransmitters – serotonin specifically – might play a role in the development of anorexia.[87]

There are several psychological risk factors for anorexia nervosa. People with anorexia are, for example, more likely than others to be high in perfectionism and low in self-esteem.[88] In addition, stress has been implicated as a risk factor for anorexia and other eating disorders – particularly stress related to interpersonal relationships – including abuse and bullying. There also are several cognitive patterns associated with anorexia and other eating disorders, including an obsession with food and eating and disordered thinking, such as believing one is fat despite clear evidence to the contrary.[89] Several of these psychological risk factors, including perfectionism, have contributed to the exacerbation of many people's eating disorders during the pandemic in an attempt to regain control.[90]

Finally, there are social and cultural influences on anorexia nervosa. For one, rates of eating disorders are higher among children of parents who themselves have disordered eating habits or who exhibit an unhealthy focus on the child's weight.[91] Relatedly, there are specific patterns of family dysfunction – such as overinvolved parents who are simultaneously highly critical – that correlate with eating disorders.[92] In addition, eating disorders – including anorexia nervosa – tend to occur in cultures where there is plenty of food available.[93]

However, probably the most discussed of the cultural and social factors is the role of the media in perpetuating a standard of beauty that involves unrealistic thinness for women in many Western countries. Evidence that images in the media play a role includes the fact that, until relatively recently, Black and Latina women had lower rates of eating disorders than White women, presumably because cultural expectations for weight were different from those among White people.[94] Regardless, the interplay of various factors is likely to be responsible. Although we are all bombarded with images of unrealistic body shapes and sizes, not all of us develops an eating disorder.[95] It is likely that biological and psychological risk factors interact with social and cultural factors in the development of anorexia nervosa and other eating disorders.

What is the typical outcome? Anorexia nervosa has one of the highest mortality rates of any psychological disorder, making it clearly a dangerous disorder.[96] People suffering from anorexia nervosa are almost 18 times as likely to die as their counterparts who do not have the disorder, either from suicide or physical complications of maintaining such an unhealthy weight.[97] It is difficult to recover from anorexia nervosa, although it is possible.

So, what do you do if a loved one has an eating disorder? The first step is for the person to get into treatment. Only about 50–60% of people with anorexia ever get any treatment, and many of these people seek treatment for another psychological disorder and not for anorexia.[98] Moreover, once in treatment, some people with anorexia nervosa do better than others. Among the factors associated with a poorer outcome are more extreme thinness, social and interpersonal problems, and more several psychological problems, including having another psychological disorder at the same time.[99,100] But recovery is possible, and we urge those who think that they or a loved one have this disorder to turn to the part of this section on how to seek help.

Part 2.6 Different mental illness treatments + effectiveness

Before we introduce you to some of the most common treatments, it's important to note that psychological treatment is not just for people with diagnosable psychological disorders. Many people seek treatment for other issues, including adjusting to new circumstances, dealing with a loss, or working on problems in relationships. Regardless of the reason for seeking help, many people receive some combination of treatments from biological, psychological, and social and cultural perspectives. It's also important to acknowledge that mental healthcare is inequitably distributed, with some people more easily able to access treatment than others. This discrepancy was particularly pronounced during the pandemic.[101,102]

Biological treatments. The primary biological treatments for psychological disorders are medications, a category called psychotropic medications.[103] We'll introduce two main classes of psychotropic medications: Antidepressants and anti-anxiety medications. There are other biological treatments aimed at affecting the brain through electrical or magnetic impulses. After we describe the main psychotropic medications, we'll introduce one of these treatments – transcranial magnetic stimulation (TcMS).

As a group, the psychotropic medications affect symptoms of psychological disorders by altering the actions of neurotransmitters, chemicals that allow neurons to communicate with one another. Researchers have pinpointed neurotransmitters that seem to play a role in the various psychological disorders, either due to a lack or surplus of that chemical.

The psychotropic medications available work in large part to alter the effects of various neurotransmitters, and many of these medications are generally effective in relieving symptoms. This description makes it sound like the process is clear cut and that researchers know exactly which neurotransmitter to tweak to achieve a perfect balance. However, that's far from the case. In most instances we don't know exactly how a given medication affects the brain.[104] In other instances, there are medications that are effective for more than one psychological disorder – often for very different psychological disorders or even for nonpsychological disorders.[105,106] On the contrary, before you get too skeptical about the science of psychotropic medications, remember that many medications for purely physical disorders suffer from these same drawbacks.

What are the most commonly prescribed psychotropic medications? As of 2018, nine out of the ten most commonly prescribed psychotropic medications in the United States targeted depression and/or anxiety.[107]

The antidepressants target the symptoms associated with depressive disorders, although they are used for many other disorders as well, including the anxiety disorders. The most common antidepressants, such as Zoloft and Lexapro, affect the neurotransmitter serotonin, although there are antidepressants that affect other neurotransmitters in addition to or instead of serotonin. The National Institute of Mental Health (NIMH) concludes that, overall, the antidepressant medications are roughly equivalent to one another in their effectiveness, but that for an individual patient, some antidepressants may work better than others.[108] So, some people end up switching antidepressants to find one that works better or leads to fewer unpleasant side effects.

Overall, antidepressants seem to be somewhat effective. After a few months of treatment, just under 30% of patients no longer meet criteria for depression; the rate climbs to about 70% after a year.[109] Some researchers, however, credit this improvement to a placebo effect. That is, these researchers believe that improvement occurs as a result of the patient's expectation that the medication will help rather than any actual biological action of the medication.[110] As evidence for this assertion, the researchers point out that the rates of improvement for antidepressants are not much higher than simply taking a placebo (or exercising, a surprisingly effective treatment for depression). However, the research on antidepressant effectiveness is inconclusive, so if you are experiencing depression, follow the guidance of your clinician.

The goal of the anti-anxiety medications, as you might guess, is to reduce symptoms associated with anxiety disorders. The most common anti-anxiety medications, such as Xanax, are benzodiazepines, which act by affecting the neurotransmitter Gamma aminobutyric acid (GABA).[111] There are several problems with benzodiazepines. One problem is that they only treat anxiety and not depression, which frequently occurs along with anxiety.[112] Second, they don't seem to be particularly effective in the long run and some researchers think they are way overprescribed.[113] Third, they can be addictive.[114] Over time, people can develop a tolerance to them and need a higher dose to achieve the same effect; some people even become dependent on them. For these reasons it is recommended that, for the most part, these medications should be used only occasionally or on a short-term basis. Cognitive-behavior therapy, discussed below, and antidepressants, discussed previously, tend to be the better choices. For panic disorder in particular, however, benzodiazepines are not a treatment of choice. The most frequently prescribed class of medications for panic disorder is the antidepressants.[115]

Transcranial magnetic stimulation or TcMS is part of a group of treatments that affect the brain through electrical or magnetic impulses and are most often used to treat depression.[116] These treatments are relatively new, and because of that not yet always covered by insurance. TcMS works by targeting a specific part of the brain with a magnetic pulse.[117] Patients typically undergo multiple rounds of treatment, each for more than a half hour.[118,119] TcMS and similar treatments are a reminder that the fields of psychology and psychiatry are continuously searching for newer and more effective treatments.

Who can treat patients using biological treatments? The main professionals who use these approaches are physicians. Although many people are treated by their general practitioners, the medical specialty with training specific to psychological disorders is psychiatry. Most psychiatrists focus exclusively on biological treatments, although some do practice psychotherapy as well.

Psychological treatments. The primary psychological treatments are the talking therapies in which an individual patient, a group of patients, a couple, or a family meets with a psychotherapist who, through conversations, aims to treat symptoms of psychological disorders and other issues that affect mental health. We'll introduce three of the primary types of psychotherapy: Psychodynamic therapy, behavioral therapy, and cognitive therapy. It's important to note that many psychotherapists describe their approach as eclectic or integrative, and use aspects of multiple treatments.[120] Regardless of the type of therapy a patient pursues, they should seek out a therapist who adheres to evidence-based techniques – that is, a type of therapy for which the effectiveness has been demonstrated through research.[121]

You may have heard of Sigmund Freud. In the late 1800s and early 1900s, Freud developed a psychoanalytic theory of human behavior that focused on urges related to aggression and sexuality, particularly as they developed in childhood. Freud postulated that we could better understand humans by mining their unconscious– the part of their mind to which they didn't have access. The type of therapy called **psychoanalysis** grew out of it, and although there are still some practicing psychoanalysts, it is not a particularly practical approach to treatment. It involves years of therapy, often every day, so is quite time-consuming and expensive. Moreover, most of Freud's ideas are not testable; that is, there's no way to develop evidence of their existence. There is, however, a modern version of psychoanalysis, called **psychodynamic therapy**. It was developed from Freud's ideas but is more focused and is typically shorter-term than Freud envisioned. Some forms of short-term psychodynamic therapy have been supported by evidence.

Psychodynamic therapies focus on helping a patient understand the emotions, cognitions, and tensions that are outside of their awareness – those that are unconscious.[122] It does this in part through an understanding of the interactions between the patient and the therapist.[123] The therapist looks for instances of transference, a phenomenon in which the patient reenacts aspects of an important interpersonal relationship with their therapist. The therapist also tries to help the patient understand any resistance to the understanding of themselves that emerges through this exploration. There is some evidence that these therapies are effective generally, particularly if they are short-term.[124,125,126] There also is evidence for its effectiveness for specific disorders, such as depression.[127,128]

Purely behavioral therapies focus on changing behavior with an emphasis on what we know about learning – classical conditioning, operant conditioning, and observational learning. One example of a behavioral technique is systematic desensitization which is often used for different kinds of anxiety, like phobias or panic disorder. Let's say you have ophidiophobia, a deep-rooted, irrational fear of snakes. Systematic desensitization could help you to learn a new conditioned pairing – snakes and relaxation, or at least tolerance – that replaces the old conditioned pairing – snakes and terror. A therapist would ask you to create a hierarchy of snake-related fears, from least scary to most. Least scary might be looking at a photo of a snake. Most scary might be sleeping with a snake in your bed. Kidding! Most scary would more likely be briefly holding a snake. With the support of a therapist, who would usually teach you cognitive and relaxation skills to help you confront your fears, you'd work systematically through these levels, building to the next one only when you were comfortable with the previous one. And newer research suggests that mixing up the order – and not just going from least to most scary – might work even better.[129]

Purely cognitive therapies focus on patients' thoughts and beliefs and attempt to change maladaptive patterns in thinking. There are a number of cognitive techniques that therapists use.[130] As one example, patients with depression might be asked to identify their automatic thoughts, which make up the sort of running monologue in our heads that accompanies our actions. Depressed people tend to have more negative automatic thoughts than nondepressed people. During a conversation with a new acquaintance at a party, for example, a depressed person's automatic thoughts may include "Everything I say sounds stupid" or "She's looking away; she's bored!" Cognitive techniques teach a depressed person to pay attention to these thoughts and challenge ones – like the examples here – that may not be adaptive.

It's relatively rare, however, that therapists implement only behavioral or only cognitive techniques. In reality, cognitive and behavioral therapies are often combined and referred to as cognitive behavioral therapy, or CBT.[131] As a combination, CBT is an effective treatment to reduce the likelihood of a relapse for depressive disorders, anxiety disorders, and several other disorders.[132] This effect is similar to or better than what is seen with medications, a finding that indicates that long-term medication may be unnecessary for many people.[133,134] For those who have access to CBT and are willing to do the work that this treatment requires, CBT seems to be a solid choice.

Who implements the psychological approaches? There are a number of professions that are licensed to treat patients using psychotherapy. Licensure varies by state within the United States, by province in Canada, as well as by country around the world, but the following are several of the professions that you are likely to encounter if you seek psychotherapy. In the United States,

Canada, and some other countries, clinical and counseling psychologists hold doctoral degrees (a Ph.D. or a Psy.D.) and are trained to treat and research psychological disorders. Licensed social workers usually are required to hold a master's degree in social work, the MSW; they typically work through an organization, but can be licensed to practice psychotherapy.

There are other types of degrees that can be licensed depending on U.S. state laws and Canadian provincial and territorial laws. These include marriage and family therapists in the United States, licensed clinical professional counsellors in Canada, and some other types of professional psychotherapists. (One important exception to this overview is that a number of regions of the world require a master's degree or equivalent to be a practicing psychologist, rather than a doctorate. Some require only a bachelor's degree. Be sure to research the laws and licensure requirements where you live.)

Social and cultural factors. Earlier we outlined the inclusion of cultural factors in the DSM-5. Cultural beliefs, expectations, and experiences can affect whether we seek treatment and, if we do, what kind of treatment we seek, as well as how we respond to and experience that treatment.[135] A good mental health clinician will ask about patients' cultural background, and will use this information when determining a diagnosis and developing a treatment plan. There's a section in the DSM-5 titled "cultural formulation" that encourages clinicians to consider cultural aspects of, among other things, patients' identities, understanding of mental illness, and understanding of treatment. This section includes a "cultural formulation interview" that clinicians may use to guide their questioning. If you seek treatment, and your clinician does not ask about your culture, feel free to bring up aspects of it that you feel are relevant to your symptoms and treatment.

Nonstandard treatments. Despite the existence of the wide range of treatments we've discussed, many people do not seek out or even have access to treatment. Some have reported that more than two-thirds of people in the United States, and particularly those from historically marginalized communities, are not treated when they have a psychological disorder.[136] The situation is worse in countries where there are fewer trained clinicians than in the United States.[137] As a result of this stark need, a number of nonstandard treatments have emerged, many supported by research and many increasingly embraced during the pandemic.[138] We'll talk about two here – treatment by people who are not trained clinicians and treatment that harnesses the vast reach of technology.

When we talk about treatment administered by people who are not trained clinicians, we don't mean someone who decides on a random Tuesday to hang a sign outside their house and advertise therapy services. Rather, we mean people who have not undergone a formal education in psychology or another licensed mental health practice, but have undergone some kind of empirically supported training. Such models are more common outside of the United States, and some have estimated that there are more than 40 million people globally who work as community mental health workers without any traditional formal training.[139]

This model, along with other community models, is a welcome innovation because there just aren't enough formally educated mental health clinicians to go around, particularly in lower-income parts of the world.[140] For the most part, lay counselors have some training despite their lack of a formal license. Many also work under supervision. For example, people running a refugee camp for Somali and Rwandan refugees in Uganda recruited members of the refugee community to serve as lay counselors.[141] The recruits underwent a brief training on how to counsel their fellow refugees with posttraumatic stress disorder, and the results were striking. About 70% of those who were treated no longer met the criteria for the diagnosis of PTSD following treatment, whereas only 40% of those who were not treated were in remission.

In the United States, there's also a long tradition of lay counselors staffing "hotlines" – whether by telephone, online, or text – to provide support for issues ranging from quitting smoking to dealing with suicidal thoughts.[142,143] But there's clearly room to expand the use of lay counselors and paraprofessionals to add to the network of psychologists, psychiatrists, and other licensed mental health clinicians to help address the enormous global need for mental healthcare, a need that increased markedly during the pandemic.

Another promising avenue for expanding care is technology. Sometimes it's old-school technology, as in the mental healthcare delivery systems commonly called eHealth or telehealth.[144,145] A patient in a rural area without a clinician may link to a trained clinician via computer – a more secure version of Zoom, essentially – or even just by old-fashioned telephone. And research suggests that eHealth therapies and in-person therapies are similarly effective.[146,147] During the pandemic, eHealth saw rapid growth; technological interventions quickly received legal authorization as in-person therapy became dangerous.[148] For reasons related to access, equity, and convenience, it seems that eHealth psychological treatments are here to stay.[149]

Beyond eHealth, however, there are a number of other innovative technology-based approaches to treatment. For example, researchers have found that virtual reality technology successfully helps expose patients to situations that lead to fear or anxiety, including specific phobias – think, handling a spider virtually to reduce arachnophobia – and posttraumatic stress disorder.[150,151,152]

More recently, researchers have developed treatments in the spirit of video games. For example, one game, SuperBetter, alleviates depression by encouraging people to work toward goals and develop stronger social support networks. The free game can be played through an app or the internet and is connected with social media and online communities, and research has supported its effectiveness.[153] There's still a need for more research on games for mental health, but nonetheless, a treatment that is free and easily accessed is, you could say, a game changer.

In recent years, and particularly during the pandemic, numerous smartphone apps have come on the market – some free and some paid.[154] But use caution, because unlike SuperBetter and several other games, most apps have not been subjected to research.[155,156] Ask whether mental health experts were involved in its development, and whether there are data on how well it works. Finally, be sure to seek input from a mental health professional if your symptoms are serious. For many people, a game or an app should be used as an addition to traditional treatment, not an alternative.

Part 2.7 What to do if I think I need treatment?

In this section, we'll offer guidance on how to find a clinician, how to get the most out of treatment, and what to do if your treatment is not working. If you're a university student, your first stop may be your university counseling center. At many institutions, therapy is free to students, or at least low cost. Plus, you're probably already on campus quite a bit, so it's likely convenient to attend appointments. Check your college or university's Web site for more information.

For the rest of us, there are several helpful online resources. To find a psychologist, you can use the locator service on the Web site of the American Psychological Association (APA) directory (locator.apa.org) or visit the "**Finding a Psychologist**" page on the Canadian Psychological Association (CPA) Web site (cpa.ca/public/findingapsychologist). If you are specifically looking for a cognitive-behavioral therapist, you can check out the psychologist finder on the Association for Behavioral and Cognitive Therapies (ABCT) which provides information for American and Canadian clinicians (findcbt.org/xFAT). For other countries, you can check the Web site of the national or regional psychological association; the APA publishes a directory of national organizations on their Web site (apa.org/international/networks/organizations/national-orgs). If you wish to seek biological treatments, you can either start with your general practitioner who may treat you or refer you to a psychiatrist. Or you can check out the directory of the relevant national association of psychiatrists. For example, in the United States, the American Psychiatric Association hosts a psychiatrist finder on its Web site (finder.psychiatry.org).

No matter how you find a clinician, you should get the answers to several important questions.

- What kind of clinician are they? Are they licensed?
- What is their approach to treatment (e.g., psychodynamic, cognitive-behavioral)? Remember, many clinicians identify as eclectic or integrative, which means they use a mix of treatments depending on the situation.
- Is the approach evidence-based? Your clinician should be able to tell you, but you can also check out the Web site of the U.S. Substance Abuse and Mental Health Services Administration (SAMHSA; samhsa.gov/resource-search/ebp), which provides information on psychological and psychiatric treatments, including a 2021 guide on telehealth. In either case, be wary of clinicians who dismiss questions about evidence.

- Is the clinician experienced in the kinds of psychological disorders or issues with which you're presenting?
- Is the clinician experienced with any relevant sociocultural aspects of your situation?
- And then the nuts and bolts. Does the clinician take your insurance? Do they handle the insurance or are you expected to pay and then seek reimbursement yourself? What will it cost you out of pocket? Does the scheduling work for you?

You wouldn't buy a new smartphone without asking a ton of questions about memory, cost, data plans/roaming, geographic coverage, and so on. Don't seek psychological or psychiatric treatment without the same kind of consumer savvy. Your mental health is that important.

Getting the most out of treatment. The U.S. Department of Health and Human Services, in conjunction with a number of other U.S. government agencies, identified ten "fundamental components of recovery." Five have to do directly with steps you can take – (1) take responsibility for the process of recovery, (2) exert control over the treatment process, (3) feel empowered to make choices about the process, (4) receive individualized treatment based on your experiences and culture, and (5) receive treatment that builds on your strengths.

The remaining five recovery components relate more directly to treatment. (6) There is a recognition that treatment must consider your whole life, and not just your current symptoms, and (7) that the recovery process is not likely to be linear; that is, there will be setbacks along the way. (8) It is important that your peers are engaged in the process so that you can all offer one another support. Finally, as part of the treatment, you should be able to expect (9) respect from your clinicians and (10) a feeling of hope from them that progress is possible. As you work to improve your mental health, keep these principles in mind and work with your clinician to be sure that your treatment is adhering to them. Remember, therapy involves two people – your therapist and you. Don't expect your therapist to magically cure you without any effort on your part.

When it's not working. If therapy is not going well, you're not stuck. Have you ever stopped streaming a movie you didn't like to switch to another, or changed barbers or hair stylists because you just didn't like how they cut your hair? People are much more likely to make a change in these arguably less important contexts than with mental healthcare. Moreover, people are more likely to change psychotropic medications than therapists if they're not improving.[157] Don't be afraid to ask for what you want, or to find a new clinician if the first one is not a good fit for you.

How do you know when to change clinicians? When you start therapy, your clinician should give you a rough timeline for treatment, and should regularly assess whether the treatment is working.[158] Ask for a timeline and information about assessments at your first visit if your therapist doesn't bring these up. If the end of the initial timeline approaches and the assessments don't indicate sufficient improvement, you have options: (1) come up with a new game plan with your current therapist, (2) add an additional clinician – a psychiatrist for medications or another therapist to do, say, couple or family therapy, or (3) ask for a referral to another therapist.[159] Too often people simply quit therapy when it's not working out. But therapy works, and you can help by being an active participant in the process, including when part of that process is changing treatments.

Part 2.8 You know someone seriously considering suicide. What should you do?

Every year, more than 800,000 people around the world die by suicide, accounting for almost 1.5% of all global deaths.[160] Although global suicide rates have generally been declining over time, the opposite is true in the United States where about 40,000 people die by suicide every year, making it the 10th most common cause of death.[161,162] (The suggested language is "die by suicide" rather than "commit suicide," because the latter makes it sound like a crime rather than the outcome of suffering and struggle.[163]) Although women in the United States are more likely than men to have suicidal thoughts, men make up about three quarters of completed suicides.[164] There also are ethnic disparities in the likelihood that someone will die by suicide, with rates higher among Latino young people and among American Indians/Alaska Natives of all ages.[165] Rates are also markedly higher in the LGBTQ+ community.[166,167]

Although there are higher rates of suicide attempts and suicide completions among certain demographic groups, it can affect anyone. And suicide is often a taboo topic. One family, after losing their 31-year-old daughter to suicide, were open about her cause of death. They hoped to ignite "a community-wide discussion about mental health and to pull the suffocating demon of depression and suicide into the bright light of day."

What would this family have us discuss? Perhaps the ways that we can identify and help people at risk for suicide. Those most at risk include people who have had a family member die by suicide, attempted suicide previously, have been diagnosed with depression, have a history of substance abuse, have recently experienced loss or other serious stressors, lack access to treatment for psychological issues, and are able to access the means to attempt suicide.[168] But there also are factors that lower the risk. These include treatment for psychological issues; social support of family and friends; and the development of problem-solving skills that help identify solutions other than suicide.[169] These researchers provide guidance to others who wish to learn more about this self-care movement.

What should you do if you or a loved one is thinking about suicide? First, don't ignore the topic. Contrary to popular belief, asking someone if they are thinking about suicide will not somehow plant that idea in their head if it wasn't already there. Second, if someone tells you that they are thinking about suicide, take them seriously. Make sure they get connected with a professional, and if they refuse to get help, tell someone who can assist you in getting them help.

There are numerous resources available to help someone who is suicidal or to offer advice to the friends and family of someone who is suicidal. In the United States, for example, you can call the National Suicide Prevention Lifeline at 1-800-273-TALK (8255). In Canada, you can visit the Web site for the organization suicide.org (suicide.org/hotlines/international/canada-suicide-hotlines.html) which provides numbers for suicide hotlines around the country. Outside the United States and Canada, you can visit the Web site for the International Association for Suicide Prevention (iasp.info/resources/Crisis_Centres) which provides information on hotlines and crisis centers around the world. *Crisis Text Line* (crisistextline.org), in which people can text with a volunteer in English or Spanish, is another resource. It's available in the United States and Canada (text 741741), Ireland (50808), and the UK (85258), and has plans to continue to expand internationally. And the Trevor Project (thetrevorproject.org), which focuses on suicide prevention among young LGBTQ+ people in the United States, also hosts an international online community (trevorspace.org). The bottom line – don't ignore the problem, and remember that social support and psychological treatment are both protective factors; the help you're giving could be life-saving.

Part 2.9 Putting it all together: Five ways to work on your psychological health

Here, we'll first highlight three areas of your life that can protect you in the face of the psychological stress you'll almost surely face in your life. We'll then introduce the concept of resilience, the remarkable ability that humans have to not only survive, but also thrive, in the face of hardship.

Stress reduction. The research on reducing stress is closely tied to the research on positive psychology. **Positive psychology** is the science that addresses the flip side of psychological disorders, stress, and the other negative issues we've talked about in this section. It offers an antidote to the historical focus on psychological problems by focusing on "hope, wisdom, creativity, future mindedness, courage, spirituality, responsibility, and perseverance" and how we can develop these qualities to enhance our psychological well-being and overall quality of life (p. 279).[170] You can read more about stress in Section 1 of this book.

So, what is in our power to do that can make us happier and help us to reduce stress? Three of the most important factors are experiencing strong support from our social networks, pursuing work or other pursuits that give meaning to our lives, and strengthening our bodies and minds. We'll explore the research backing each of these areas, in turn.

Social support appears to be an important pathway by which we use our psychological reserves to increase our overall well-being.[171] Some researchers believe that social support is helpful because our network both provides very real assistance when we need help coping and is there for us as emotional support, displaying understanding and caring in times of stress.[172] Even marriage, long the punch line for what supposedly makes us *un*happy, actually tends to make people happier.[173] Our advice: To the degree that it is possible, prioritize your relationships, particularly those in which you feel cared for and supported.

A second key to psychological well-being is feeling that our lives have meaning, that our lives "matter in some larger sense."[174] This can include a general tendency to find meaning in stressful or traumatic events, or just in everyday life. Employment, for example, can have meaning, particularly when we can see the greater purpose of the work that we do and the organization for which we work.[175] It's wonderful when our jobs have meaning; however, that won't be the case for all of us. That's why it's important to also seek meaning elsewhere, with families and friends, through hobbies or athletic pursuits, through religion or other spiritual pursuits, or in volunteer work.[176,177] Life can change; we may lose our jobs or develop relationship problems, for example, which is why it's important to spread out the sources of our experiences of meaning.[178]

A third way to improve our psychological well-being is to focus on our bodies and minds. A great deal of research has found that physical exercise improves mood, self-esteem, resilience in the face of stress, and overall psychological well-being.[179] There's also evidence that exercise helps reduce the symptoms of those who have been diagnosed with anxiety and depressive disorders.[180] Why is exercise good for us psychologically? Researchers have postulated biological mechanisms, including increases in endorphins and changes in other neurotransmitters, as well as psychological mechanisms, such as the feeling of accomplishment that often accompanies exercise.[181] Regardless of the reason, exercise is great for us psychologically as well as physically.

There are also benefits to taking care of our minds, including through mindfulness, often practiced through meditation. Mindfulness consists of developing an awareness of our bodily sensations, emotions, thoughts, and immediate environment, and then working to accept these internal and external experiences in a nonjudgmental way.[182] Mindfulness can be practiced through more formal practices like meditation and yoga, but also more informally, such as through immersion in art and nature.

Researchers have shared that meditation generally and mindfulness in particular lead to lower levels of depression, anxiety, and stress, on average, and higher levels of psychological well-being.[183,184] If you've never tried practicing mindfulness, here's a Web site from the University of California Los Angeles that provides several free audio (or visual) exercises in more than a dozen languages, including English, Spanish, and American Sign Language that you can follow to at home: marc.ucla.edu/body.cfm?id=22. You can also do an online search for "free mindfulness meditation."

Finally, we can combine attention to our bodies and minds by taking advantage of the meditative qualities of the natural environment, something that researchers call "green exercise."[185] It turns out that just being in green spaces is good for our mental health. One large study reported benefits for people's mood and self-esteem in wilderness environments like forests, rural environments like farms, and even in green urban environments like leafy parks, with enhanced benefits in the presence of water, like a river or a lake.[186] Amazingly, benefits are evident after just five minutes surrounded by nature! So, make it a daily habit to take even a short walk through a nearby park, and perhaps practice mindfulness while you do.

Resilience. Even if we experience particularly stressful, or even traumatic, situations – as most of us will at some point in our lives – psychological disorders are not a foregone conclusion. We humans are remarkably resilient, including after difficult and potentially traumatic life events, such as divorce or unemployment, and following traumas, such as combat or assault. We so often talk about posttraumatic stress. Yet, many people experience the flip side of that – posttraumatic growth.[187]

Posttraumatic growth refers to the sometimes-substantial positive changes that some people report experiencing in response to traumatic events. More and more we realize that traumatic events need not be precursors to psychological disorders – or even to long-term psychological symptoms.[188] The positive outcomes of a traumatic event can take a number of forms, including becoming a stronger person psychologically, perceiving previously unseen possibilities in life, developing better relationships with others, becoming more appreciative of life, and growing in a spiritual, religious, or philosophical sense.[189] Posttraumatic growth can even occur alongside symptoms of posttraumatic stress, which means that even those with negative responses to stress may still have positive outcomes long-term.[190]

A final word on stigma. We hope this section has given you a sense of what psychological disorders are and how they are treated, and that this understanding will help you weather the psychological storms that many of us will encounter in our lives. But we also hope that you won't shy away from the kinds of conversations that can bring mental illness out of the darkness and allow us to work together as individuals and societies to identify those who are suffering and provide them with equitable access to treatment.

Notes

1   Finster, H. (1989). *Howard Finster: Man of visions.* Peachtree Publishers.
2   Turner, J. (1989). *Howard Finster: Man of visions.* Knopf.
3   Rosenbaum, A. (n.d.). *Howard Finster (ca. 1915–2001).* www.georgiaencyclopedia.org/articles/arts-culture/howard-finster-ca-1915-2001
4   Associated Press. (2007). *Home turned into a museum honors folk artist.* www.nbcnews.com/id/22100056/ns/travel-destination_travel/t/home-turned-museum-honors-folk-artist/#.VrjtetwrJD8
5   Hunter, M. (2015). *Finster's 'paradise': The south's most inspired garden.* www.cnn.com/2014/11/12/travel/paradise-garden-howard-finster/index.html
6   Comer, R. J. (2019). *Fundamentals of abnormal psychology.* Macmillan.
7   First, M. B., & Wakefield, J. C. (2010). Defining "mental disorder" in DSM-V. *Psychological Medicine, 40*(11), 1779–1782.

8 Smink, F. R., Van Hoeken, D., & Hoek, H. W. (2012). Epidemiology of eating disorders: Incidence, prevalence and mortality rates. *Current Psychiatry Reports*, 14(4), 406–414.

9 Kessler, R. C., Angermeyer, M., Anthony, J. C., De Graaf, R., Demyttenaere, K., Gasquet, I., ... & Kawakami, N. (2007). Lifetime prevalence and age-of-onset distributions of mental disorders in the World Health Organization's World Mental Health Survey Initiative. *World Psychiatry*, 6(3), 168–176.

10 NIMH. (2015). *Any mental illness (AMI) among U.S. adults*. National Institute of Mental Health. www.nimh.nig.gov/health/statistics/prevalence/any-mental-illness-ami-among-us-adults-shtml.

11 Limcaoco, G. R. S., Mateos, E. M., Fernández, J. M., & Roncero, C. (2020). Anxiety, worry and perceived stress in the world due to the COVID-19 pandemic, March 2020. Preliminary results. *MedRxiv*. https://doi.org/10.1101/2020.04.03.20043992

12 Wu, T., Jia, X., Shi, H., Jieqiong, N., Xiaohan, Y., Xie, J., & Wang, X. (2021). Prevalence of mental health problems during the COVID-19 pandemic: A systematic review and meta-analysis. *Elsevier*, 281, 91–98. https://doi.org/10.1016/j.jad.2020.11.117

13 Krishnamoorthy, Y., Nagarajan, R., Saya, G. K., & Menon, V. (2020). Prevalence of psychological morbidities among general population, healthcare workers and COVID-19 patients amidst the COVID-19 pandemic: A systematic review and meta-analysis. *Psychiatry Research*, 293, 113382. https://doi.org/10.1016/j.psychres.2020.113382

14 American Psychiatric Association. (2013). *Diagnostic and statistical manual of mental disorders* (5th ed.). American Psychiatric Association.

15 World Health Organization. (2016). *International statistical classification of diseases and related health problems* (10th rev.). http://apps.who.int/classifications/icd10/browse/2016/en

16 American Psychiatric Association. (2013). *Diagnostic and statistical manual of mental disorders* (5th ed.). American Psychiatric Association.

17 Kraemer, H. C. (2015). Research domain criteria (RDoC) and the DSM – Two methodological approaches to mental health diagnosis. *JAMA Psychiatry*, 72(12), 1163–1164.

18 Frances, A. J., & Nardo, J. M. (2013). ICD-11 should not repeat the mistakes made by DSM-5. *The British Journal of Psychiatry*, 203(1), 1–2.

19 Cosgrove, L., & Krimsky, S. (2012). A comparison of DSM-IV and DSM-5 panel members' financial associations with industry: a pernicious problem persists. *PLoS Med*, 9(3), e1001190.

20 Rose, D., Thornicroft, G., Pinfold, V., & Kassam, A. (2007). 250 labels used to stigmatise people with mental illness. *BMC Health Services Research*, 7, 1–7.

21 Beck, A. T., Emery, G., & Greenberg, R. L. (2005). *Anxiety disorders and phobias: A cognitive perspective*. Basic Books.

22 Low, G., Kalfoss, M., & Halvorsrud, L. (2015). Identity processes, depression, and the aging self – A Norwegian study. *Advances in Aging Research*, 4(6), 212–224.

23 Foa, E. B., Stein, D. J., & McFarlane, A. C. (2006). Symptomatology and psychopathology of mental health problems after disaster. *Journal of Clinical Psychiatry*, 67, 15–25.

24 American Psychological Association. (2009). *ICD vs. DSM*. www.apa.org/monitor/2009/10/icd-dsm.aspx

25 Bowen, F. (2021, 10 June). Tennis star Naomi Osaka revealed mental health struggles many people face. *Washington Post*. www.washingtonpost.com/lifestyle/kidspost/tennis-star-naomi-osaka-revealed-mental-health-struggles-many-people-face/2021/06/09/d4276d14-c3e5-11eb-9a8d-f95d7724967c_story.html

26 Zung, W. W. (1965). A self-rating depression scale. *Archives of General Psychiatry*, *12*, 63–70.

27 Dunstan, D. A., Scott, N., & Todd, A. K. (2017). Screening for anxiety and depression: Reassessing the utility of the Zung scales. *BMC Psychiatry*, *17*(1), 1–8. https://doi.org/10.1186/s12888-017-1489-6

28 Kessler, R. C., Berglund, P., Demler, O., Jin, R., Merikangas, K. R., & Walters, E. E. (2005). Lifetime prevalence and age-of-onset distributions of DSM-IV disorders in the National Comorbidity Survey Replication. *Archives of General Psychiatry*, *62*, 593–602.

29 Ferrari, A. J., Somerville, A. J., Baxter, A. J., Norman, R., Patten, S. B., Vos, T., & Whiteford, H. A. (2013). Global variation in the prevalence and incidence of major depressive disorder: A systematic review of the epidemiological literature. *Psychological Medicine*, *43*(3), 471–481.

30 Kessler, R. C., Berglund, P., Demler, O., Jin, R., Koretz, D., Merikangas, K. R., … & Wang, P. S. (2003). The epidemiology of major depressive disorder: Results from the National Comorbidity Survey Replication (NCS-R). *JAMA*, *289*(23), 3095–3105.

31 Nolen-Hoeksema, S. (2001). Gender differences in depression. *Current Directions in Psychological Science*, *10*(5), 173–176.

32 Beck, A. T., & Bredemeier, K. (2016). A unified model of depression integrating clinical, cognitive, biological, and evolutionary perspectives. *Clinical Psychological Science*, *4*(4), 596–619.

33 Kendler, K. S., Gatz, M., Gardner, C. O., & Pedersen, N. L. (2006). A Swedish national twin study of lifetime major depression. *American Journal of Psychiatry*, *163*(1), 109–114.

34 Holmans, P., Weissman, M. M., Zubenko, G. S., Scheftner, W. A., Crowe, R. R., DePaulo Jr, J. R., … & Boutelle, S. (2007). Genetics of recurrent early-onset major depression (GenRED): Final genome scan report. *American Journal of Psychiatry*, *164*(2), 248–258.

35 Werner, F. M., & Coveñas, R. (2013). Classical neurotransmitters and neuropeptides involved in major depression in a multi-neurotransmitter system: A focus on antidepressant drugs. *Current Medicinal Chemistry*, *20*(38), 4853–4858.

36 Sacher, J., Neumann, J., Fünfstück, T., Soliman, A., Villringer, A., & Schroeter, M. L. (2012). Mapping the depressed brain: A meta-analysis of structural and functional alterations in major depressive disorder. *Journal of Affective Disorders*, *140*(2), 142–148.

37 Groenewold, N. A., Opmeer, E. M., de Jonge, P., Aleman, A., & Costafreda, S. G. (2013). Emotional valence modulates brain functional abnormalities in depression: Evidence from a meta-analysis of fMRI studies. *Neuroscience & Biobehavioral Reviews*, *37*(2), 152–163.

38 Cohen, S., Janicki-Deverts, D., & Miller, G. E. (2007). Psychological stress and disease. *JAMA*, *298*(14), 1685–1687.

39 Lupien, S. J., McEwen, B. S., Gunnar, M. R., & Heim, C. (2009). Effects of stress throughout the lifespan on the brain, behaviour and cognition. *Nature Reviews Neuroscience*, *10*(6), 434–445.

40 Human Rights Watch (2020, 12 May). *COVID-19 fueling anti-Asian racism and xenophobia worldwide.* www.hrw.org/news/2020/05/12/covid-19-fueling-anti-asian-racism-and-xenophobia-worldwide

41 Burke, H. M., Davis, M. C., Otte, C., & Mohr, D. C. (2005). Depression and cortisol responses to psychological stress: A meta-analysis. *Psychoneuroendocrinology*, 30(9), 846–856.

42 Plant, E. A., & Sachs-Ericsson, N. (2004). Racial and ethnic differences in depression: The roles of social support and meeting basic needs. *Journal of Consulting and Clinical Psychology*, 72(1), 41–52.

43 Ferrari, A. J., Somerville, A. J., Baxter, A. J., Norman, R., Patten, S. B., Vos, T., & Whiteford, H. A. (2013). Global variation in the prevalence and incidence of major depressive disorder: A systematic review of the epidemiological literature. *Psychological Medicine*, 43(3), 471–481

44 Kessler, R. C., Berglund, P., Demler, O., Jin, R., Koretz, D., Merikangas, K. R., … & Wang, P. S. (2003). The epidemiology of major depressive disorder: Results from the National Comorbidity Survey Replication (NCS-R). *JAMA*, 289(23), 3095–3105.

45 Vittengl, J. R., Clark, L. A., Dunn, T. W., & Jarrett, R. B. (2007). Reducing relapse and recurrence in unipolar depression: A comparative meta-analysis of cognitive-behavioral therapy's effects. *Journal of Consulting and Clinical Psychology*, 75(3), 475–488.

46 Kovacs, M., Obrosky, S., & George, C. (2016). The course of major depressive disorder from childhood to young adulthood: Recovery and recurrence in a longitudinal observational study. *Journal of Affective Disorders*, 203, 374–381.

47 Kessing, L. V., Hansen, M. G., Andersen, P. K., & Angst, J. (2004). The predictive effect of episodes on the risk of recurrence in depressive and bipolar disorders–A lifelong perspective. *Acta Psychiatrica Scandinavica*, 109(5), 339–344.

48 Kohn, R., Saxena, S., Levav, I., & Saraceno, B. (2004). The treatment gap in mental health care. *Bulletin of the World Health Organization*, 82(11), 858–866.

49 Wang, P. S., Berglund, P., Olfson, M., Pincus, H. A., Wells, K. B., & Kessler, R. C. (2005). Failure and delay in initial treatment contact after first onset of mental disorders in the National Comorbidity Survey Replication. *Archives of General Psychiatry*, 62(6), 603–613.

50 Cuijpers, P., Noma, H., Karyotaki, E., Vinkers, C. H., Cipriani, A., & Furukawa, T. A. (2020). A network meta-analysis of the effects of psychotherapies, pharmacotherapies and their combination in the treatment of adult depression. *World Psychiatry*, 19(1), 92–107. https://doi.org/10.1002/wps.20701

51 Baskin, K. (2012). *Panic in paradise.* http://opinionator.blogs.nytimes.com/2012/03/31/panic-in-paradise/#more-125807

52 Baskin, K. (2012). *Panic in paradise.* http://opinionator.blogs.nytimes.com/2012/03/31/panic-in-paradise/#more-125807. Para. 5

53 Zung, W. W. (1971). A rating instrument for anxiety disorders. *Psychosomatics*, 12(6), 371–379. https://doi.org/10.1016/S0033-3182(71)71479-0

54 Dunstan, D. A., Scott, N., & Todd, A. K. (2017). Screening for anxiety and depression: Reassessing the utility of the Zung scales. *BMC Psychiatry*, 17(1), 1–8. https://doi.org/10.1186/s12888-017-1489-6

55 Baskin, K. (2012). *Panic in paradise.* http://opinionator.blogs.nytimes.com/2012/03/31/panic-in-paradise/#more-125807. Para

56 Whiteford, H. A., Degenhardt, L., Rehm, J., Baxter, A. J., Ferrari, A. J., Erskine, H. E., … & Burstein, R. (2013). Global burden of disease attributable to mental

and substance use disorders: Findings from the Global Burden of Disease Study 2010. *The Lancet, 382*(9904), 1575–1586.

57 Kessler, R. C., Berglund, P., Demler, O., Jin, R., Merikangas, K. R., & Walters, E. E. (2005). Lifetime prevalence and age-of-onset distributions of DSM-IV disorders in the National Comorbidity Survey Replication. *Archives of General Psychiatry, 62*(6), 593–602.

58 Kessler, R. C., Angermeyer, M., Anthony, J. C., De Graaf, R., Demyttenaere, K., Gasquet, I., … & Kawakami, N. (2007). Lifetime prevalence and age-of-onset distributions of mental disorders in the World Health Organization's World Mental Health Survey Initiative. *World Psychiatry, 6*(3), 168–176.

59 Jorm, A. F. (2000). Does old age reduce the risk of anxiety and depression? A review of epidemiological studies across the adult life span. *Psychological Medicine, 30*(1), 11–22.

60 Maron, E., Hettema, J. M., & Shlik, J. (2010). Advances in molecular genetics of panic disorder. *Molecular Psychiatry, 15*(7), 681–701.

61 Moreno-Peral, P., Conejo-Cerón, S., Motrico, E., Rodríguez-Morejón, A., Fernández, A., García-Campayo, J., … & Bellón, J. Á. (2014). Risk factors for the onset of panic and generalised anxiety disorders in the general adult population: A systematic review of cohort studies. *Journal of Affective Disorders, 168*, 337–348.

62 Del-Ben, C. M., & Graeff, F. G. (2009). Panic disorder: Is the PAG involved? *Neural plasticity*, Article ID 108135. https://doi.org/10.1155/2009/108135

63 Osma López, J. J., Barrada, J. R., García Palacios, A., & Botella Arbona, C. (2016). Influence of vulnerability factors in panic disorder severity. *Psicothema, 28*(2), 167–173. https://doi.org/10.7334/psicothema2015.223

64 Liu, Y., Sareen, J., Bolton, J., & Wang, J. (2015). Development and validation of a risk-prediction algorithm for the recurrence of panic disorder. *Depression and Anxiety, 32*(5), 341–348.

65 Liu, Y., Sareen, J., Bolton, J., & Wang, J. (2015). Development and validation of a risk-prediction algorithm for the recurrence of panic disorder. *Depression and Anxiety, 32*(5), 341–348.

66 Moreno-Peral, P., Conejo-Cerón, S., Motrico, E., Rodríguez-Morejón, A., Fernández, A., García-Campayo, J., … & Bellón, J. Á. (2014). Risk factors for the onset of panic and generalised anxiety disorders in the general adult population: A systematic review of cohort studies. *Journal of Affective Disorders, 168*, 337–348.

67 David, D., Cristea, I., & Hofmann, S. G. (2018). Why cognitive behavioral therapy is the current gold standard of psychotherapy. *Frontiers in Psychiatry, 9*, 1–3. https://doi.org/10.3389/fpsyt.2018.00004

68 Van Apeldoorn, F. J., Van Hout, W. J., Timmerman, M. E., Mersch, P. P. A., & den Boer, J. A. (2013). Rate of improvement during and across three treatments for panic disorder with or without agoraphobia: Cognitive behavioral therapy, selective serotonin reuptake inhibitor or both combined. *Journal of Affective Disorders, 150*, 313–319.

69 Barlow, D. H., Gorman, J. M., Shear, M. K., & Woods, S. W. (2000). Cognitive-behavioral therapy, imipramine, or their combination for panic disorder: A randomized controlled trial. *JAMA, 283*(19), 2529–2536.

70 Hofmann, S. G., & Smits, J. A. (2008). Cognitive-behavioral therapy for adult anxiety disorders: A meta-analysis of randomized placebo-controlled trials. *The Journal of Clinical Psychiatry, 69*(4), 621–632.

71 Norton, P. J., & Price, E. C. (2007). A meta-analytic review of adult cognitive-behavioral treatment outcome across the anxiety disorders. *The Journal of Nervous and Mental Disease, 195*(6), 521–531.

72 Schmidt, N. B., & Keough, M. E. (2010). Treatment of panic. *Annual Review of Clinical Psychology*, 6, 241–256.

73 Kohn, R., Saxena, S., Levav, I., & Saraceno, B. (2004). The treatment gap in mental health care. *Bulletin of the World Health Organization*, 82, 858–866.

74 Wang, P. S., Berglund, P., Olfson, M., Pincus, H. A., Wells, K. B., & Kessler, R. C. (2005). Failure and delay in initial treatment contact after first onset of mental disorders in the National Comorbidity Survey Replication. *Archives of General Psychiatry*, 62(6), 603–613.

75 Wolf, A. W., & Goldfried, M. R. (2014). Clinical experiences in using cognitive-behavior therapy to treat panic disorder. *Behavior Therapy*, 45(1), 36–46.

76 Waldman, K. (2015). *We need to reject the false narratives around Anorexia. I can start by telling my story.* www.slate.com/articles/double_x/cover_story/2015/12/we_need_to_reject_the_false_narratives_around_anorexia.html. Para. 54.

77 Waldman (2015), Para. 93.

78 Garner, D. M., Olmsted, M. P., Bohr, Y., & Garfinkel, P. E. (1982). The eating attitudes test: Psychometric features and clinical correlates. *Psychological Medicine*, 12(8), 871–878.

79 Hoek, H. W., & Van Hoeken, D. (2003). Review of the prevalence and incidence of eating disorders. *International Journal of Eating Disorders*, 34(4), 383–396.

80 Preti, A., de Girolamo, G., Vilagut, G., Alonso, J., de Graaf, R., Bruffaerts, R., … & ESEMeD-WMH Investigators. (2009). The epidemiology of eating disorders in six European countries: Results of the ESEMeD-WMH project. *Journal of Psychiatric Research*, 43(14), 1125–1132.

81 Sweeting, H., Walker, L., MacLean, A., Patterson, C., Räisänen, U., & Hunt, K. (2015). Prevalence of eating disorders in males: A review of rates reported in academic research and UK mass media. *International Journal of Men's Health*, 14(2), 86–112.

82 Preti, A., de Girolamo, G., Vilagut, G., Alonso, J., de Graaf, R., Bruffaerts, R., … & ESEMeD-WMH Investigators. (2009). The epidemiology of eating disorders in six European countries: Results of the ESEMeD-WMH project. *Journal of Psychiatric Research*, 43(14), 1125–1132.

83 McClain, Z., & Peebles, R. (2016). Body image and eating disorders among lesbian, gay, bisexual, and transgender youth. *Pediatric Clinics*, 63(6), 1079–1090. https://doi.org/10.1016/j.pcl.2016.07.008

84 Hudson, J. I., Hiripi, E., Pope, H. G., & Kessler, R. C. (2007). The prevalence and correlates of eating disorders in the National Comorbidity Survey Replication. *Biological Psychiatry*, 61(3), 348–358.

85 Trace, S. E., Baker, J. H., Peñas-Lledó, E., & Bulik, C. M. (2013). The genetics of eating disorders. *Annual Review of Clinical Psychology*, 9, 589–620.

86 Mazzeo, S. E., & Bulik, C. M. (2009). Environmental and genetic risk factors for eating disorders: What the clinician needs to know. *Child and Adolescent Psychiatric Clinics of North America*, 18(1), 67–82.

87 Polivy, J., & Herman, C. P. (2002). Causes of eating disorders. *Annual Review of Psychology*, 53, 187–213.

88 Mazzeo, S. E., & Bulik, C. M. (2009). Environmental and genetic risk factors for eating disorders: What the clinician needs to know. *Child and Adolescent Psychiatric Clinics of North America*, 18(1), 67–82.

89 Polivy, J., & Herman, C. P. (2002). Causes of eating disorders. *Annual Review of Psychology*, 53, 187–213.

90 Schlegl, S., Maier, J., Meule, A., & Voderholzer, U. (2020). Eating disorders in times of the COVID-19 pandemic – Results from an online survey of patients with anorexia nervosa. *International Journal of Eating Disorders*, 53(11), 1791–1800. https://doi.org/10.1002/eat.23374

91 Mazzeo, S. E., & Bulik, C. M. (2009). Environmental and genetic risk factors for eating disorders: What the clinician needs to know. *Child and Adolescent Psychiatric Clinics of North America*, 18(1), 67–82.

92 Polivy, J., & Herman, C. P. (2002). Causes of eating disorders. *Annual Review of Psychology*, 53, 187–213.

93 Polivy & Herman (2002).

94 Polivy & Herman (2002).

95 Mazzeo, S. E., & Bulik, C. M. (2009). Environmental and genetic risk factors for eating disorders: What the clinician needs to know. *Child and Adolescent Psychiatric Clinics of North America*, 18(1), 67–82.

96 Arcelus, J., Mitchell, A. J., Wales, J., & Nielsen, S. (2011). Mortality rates in patients with anorexia nervosa and other eating disorders: A meta-analysis of 36 studies. *Archives of General Psychiatry*, 68(7), 724–731. https://doi.org/10.1001/archgenpsychiatry.2011.74.

97 Steinhausen H.-C. (2009). Outcome of eating disorders. *Child and Adolescent Psychiatry Clinics of North America*, 18(1), 225–242.

98 Hudson, J. I., Hiripi, E., Pope, H. G., & Kessler, R. C. (2007). The prevalence and correlates of eating disorders in the National Comorbidity Survey Replication. *Biological Psychiatry*, 61(3), 348–358.

99 Löwe, B., Zipfel, S., Buchholz, C., Dupont, Y., Reas, D. L., & Herzog, W. (2001). Long-term outcome of anorexia nervosa in a prospective 21-year follow-up study. *Psychological Medicine*, 31(5), 881–890.

100 Mustelin, L., Raevuori, A., Bulik, C. M., Rissanen, A., Hoek, H. W., Kaprio, J., & Keski-Rahkonen, A. (2015). Long-term outcome in anorexia nervosa in the community. *International Journal of Eating Disorders*, 48(7), 851–859.

101 Altiraifi, A., & Rapfogel, N. (2020). *Mental health care was severely inequitable, then came the coronavirus crisis*. Center for American Progress. www.americanprogress.org/issues/disability/reports/2020/09/10/490221/mental-health-care-severely-inequitable-came-coronavirus-crisis/

102 Kola, L. (2020). Global mental health and COVID-19. *The Lancet Psychiatry*, 7(8), 655–657. https://doi.org/10.1016/S2215-0366(20)30235-2

103 Advokat, C. D., Comaty, J. E., & Julien, R. M. (2019). *Julien's primer of drug action: A comprehensive guide to the actions, uses, and side effects of psychoactive drugs*. Worth Publishers.

104 McLoughlin, G. A., Ma, D., Tsang, T. M., Jones, D. N., Cilia, J., Hill, M. D., … & Bahn, S. (2009). Analyzing the effects of psychotropic drugs on metabolite profiles in rat brain using 1H NMR spectroscopy. *Journal of Proteome Research*, 8(4), 1943–1952.

105 Centers for Medicare & Medicaid Services. (2015). *Antidepressant medications: Use in adults*. www.cms.gov/Medicare-Medicaid-Coordination/Fraud-Prevention/Medicaid-Integrity-Education/Pharmacy-Education-Materials/Downloads/ad-adult-factsheet11-14.pdf

106 National Institute of Mental Health. (2016). *Mental health medications*. www.nimh.nih.gov/health/topics/mental-health-medications/index.shtml

107 Grohol, J. M. (2019). *Top 25 psychiatric medication prescriptions for 2018*. https://psychcentral.com/blog/top-25-psychiatric-medications-for-2018?c=48284 5273022.

108 National Institute of Mental Health (2016). *Mental health medications.* www. nimh.nih.gov/health/topics/mental-health-medications/index.shtml

109 Insel, T. R., & Wang, P. S. (2009). The STAR* D trial: Revealing the need for better treatments. *Psychiatric Services, 60*(11), 1466–1467.

110 Khan, A., & Brown, W. A. (2015). Antidepressants versus placebo in major depression: An overview. *World Psychiatry, 14*(3), 294–300.

111 National Institute of Mental Health (2016). *Mental health medications.* www. nimh.nih.gov/health/topics/mental-health-medications/index.shtml

112 Dell'Osso, B., & Lader, M. (2013). Do benzodiazepines still deserve a major role in the treatment of psychiatric disorders? A critical reappraisal. *European Psychiatry, 28*(1), 7–20.

113 Lader, M. (2008). Effectiveness of benzodiazepines: Do they work or not? *Expert Review of Neurotherapeutics, 8*(8), 1189–1191.

114 Dell'Osso, B., & Lader, M. (2013). Do benzodiazepines still deserve a major role in the treatment of psychiatric disorders? A critical reappraisal. *European Psychiatry, 28*(1), 7–20.

115 National Institute of Mental Health (2016). *Mental health medications.* www. nimh.nih.gov/health/topics/mental-health-medications/index.shtml

116 Gelenberg, A. J., Freeman, F. P., Markowitz, J. C., Rosenbaum, J. F., Thase, M. E., Trivedi, M. H., & Van Rhoads, R. S. (2010). *Practice guideline for the treatment of patients with major depressive disorder.* http://psychiatryonline.org/pb/assets/raw/ sitewide/practice_guidelines/guidelines/mdd.pdf

117 Gelenberg et al. (2010).

118 Smith, A. (2010). *Transcranial magnetic stimulation treats depression, gains favor among psychiatrists.* http://blog.syracuse.com/cny/2010/10/transcranial_magnetic_ stimulation_treats_depression_gains_favor_among_psychiatrists.html

119 Gelenberg, A. J., Freeman, F. P., Markowitz, J. C., Rosenbaum, J. F., Thase, M. E., Trivedi, M. H., & Van Rhoads, R. S. (2010). *Practice guideline for the treatment of patients with major depressive disorder.* http://psychiatryonline.org/pb/assets/raw/ sitewide/practice_guidelines/guidelines/mdd.pdf

120 Wachtel, P. L., Siegel, J. P., & Baer, J. C. (2020). The scope of psychotherapy integration: Introduction to a special issue. *Clinical Social Work Journal, 48,* 231–235. https://doi.org/10.1007/s10615-020-00771-y

121 Barlow, D. H., Bullis, J. R., Comer, J. S., & Ametaj, A. A. (2013). Evidence-based psychological treatments: An update and a way forward. *Annual Review of Clinical Psychology, 9,* 1–27. https://doi.org/10.1146/annurev-clinpsy-050212-185629

122 Driessen, E., Cuijpers, P., de Maat, S. C., Abbass, A. A., de Jonghe, F., & Dekker, J. J. (2010). The efficacy of short-term psychodynamic psychotherapy for depression: A meta-analysis. *Clinical Psychology Review, 30*(1), 25–36.

123 Leichsenring, F., & Rabung, S. (2008). Effectiveness of long-term psychodynamic psychotherapy: A meta-analysis. *JAMA, 300*(13), 1551–1565.

124 Gerber, A. J., Kocsis, J. H., Milrod, B. L., Roose, S. P., Barber, J. P., Thase, M. E., … & Leon, A. C. (2011). A quality-based review of randomized controlled trials of psychodynamic psychotherapy. *American Journal of Psychiatry, 168*(1), 19–28.

125 Leichsenring, F., Rabung, S., & Leibing, E. (2004). The efficacy of short-term psychodynamic psychotherapy in specific psychiatric disorders: A meta-analysis. *Archives of General Psychiatry, 61*(12), 1208–1216.

126 Leichsenring, F. (2001). Comparative effects of short-term psychodynamic psychotherapy and cognitive-behavioral therapy in depression: A meta-analytic approach. *Clinical Psychology Review, 21,* 401–419.

127 Driessen, E., Hegelmaier, L. M., Abbass, A. A., Barber, J. P., Dekker, J. J., Van, H. L., … & Cuijpers, P. (2015). The efficacy of short-term psychodynamic psychotherapy for depression: A meta-analysis update. *Clinical Psychology Review*, *42*, 1–15.

128 Leichsenring, F. (2001). Comparative effects of short-term psychodynamic psychotherapy and cognitive-behavioral therapy in depression: A meta-analytic approach. *Clinical Psychology Review*, *21*(3), 401–419.

129 Knowles, K. A., & Olatunji, B. O. (2019). Enhancing inhibitory learning: The utility of variability in exposure. *Cognitive and Behavioral Practice*, *26*(1), 186–200. https://doi.org/10.1016/j.cbpra.2017.12.001

130 Beck, J. S. (2011). *Cognitive behavior therapy: Basics and beyond* (2nd ed.). Guilford Press.

131 Beck (2011).

132 Hofmann, S. G., Asnaani, A., Vonk, I. J. J., Sawyer, A. T., & Fang, A. (2012). The efficacy of cognitive behavioral therapy: A review of meta-analyses. *Cognitive Therapy and Research*, *36*(5), 427–440. http://doi.org/10.1007/s10608-012-9476-1

133 Hollon, S. D., Stewart, M. O., & Strunk, D. (2006). Enduring effects for cognitive behavior therapy in the treatment of depression and anxiety. *Annual Review of Psychology*, *57*, 285–315.

134 DeRubeis R. J., Hollon S. D., Amsterdam J. D., Shelton, R. C., Young, P. R., Salomon, R. M., … & Gallop, R. (2005). Cognitive therapy vs medications in the treatment of moderate to severe depression. *Archives of General Psychiatry*, *62*(4), 409–416. https://doi.org/10.1001/archpsyc.62.4.409.

135 Clauss-Ehlers, C. S., Chiriboga, D. A., Hunter, S. J., Roysircar, G., & Tummala-Narra, P. (2019). APA multicultural guidelines executive summary: Ecological approach to context, identity, and intersectionality. *American Psychologist*, *74*(2), 232–244. https://doi.org/10.1037/amp0000382

136 Kazdin, A. E., & Blase, S. (2011). Rebooting psychotherapy research and practice to reduce the burden of mental illness. *Perspectives on Psychological Science*, *6*(1), 21–37. https://doi.org/10.1177/1745691610393527

137 Jacob, K. S., & Patel, V. (2014). Classification of mental disorders: A global mental health perspective. *Lancet*, *383*(9926), 1433–1435. https://doi.org/10.1016/S0140-6736(13)62382-X

138 Kola, L. (2020). Global mental health and COVID-19. *The Lancet Psychiatry*, *7*(8), 655–657. https://doi.org/10.1016/S2215-0366(20)30235-2

139 Rotheram-Borus, M. J., Swendeman, D., & Chorpita, B. F. (2012). Disruptive innovations for designing and diffusing evidence-based interventions. *American Psychologist*, *67*(6), 463–476. https://doi.org/10.1037/a0028180

140 Kohrt, B. A., Asher, L., Bhardwaj, A., Fazel, M., Jordans, M. J. D., Mutamba, B. B., … & Patel, V. (2018). The role of communities in mental health care in low- and middle-income countries: A meta-review of components and competencies. *International Journal of Environmental Research and Public Health*, *15*(6), 1–31. https://doi.org/10.3390/ijerph15061279

141 Neuner, F., Onyut, P. L., Ertl, V., Odenwald, M., Schauer, E., & Elbert, T. (2008). Treatment of posttraumatic stress disorder by trained lay counselors in an African refugee settlement: A randomized controlled trial. *Journal of Consulting and Clinical Psychology*, *76*(4), 686–694. https://doi.org/10.1037/0022-006X.76.4.686

142 Kazdin, A. E., & Blase, S. (2011). Rebooting psychotherapy research and practice to reduce the burden of mental illness. *Perspectives on Psychological Science*, *6*(1), 21–37. https://doi.org/10.1177/1745691610393527

143 Lublin, N. (2013). *Crisis text line*. www.crisistextline.org

144 Teachman, B. A. (2014). No appointment necessary: Treating mental illness outside the therapist's office. *Perspectives on Psychological Science*, 9(1), 85–87. https://doi.org/10.1177/1745691613512659

145 Zhou, X., Snoswell, C. L., Harding, L. E., Bambling, M., Edirippulige, S., Bai, X., & Smith, A. C. (2020). The role of telehealth in reducing the mental health burden from COVID-19. *Telemedicine and e-Health*, 26(4), 377–379. https://doi.org/10.1089/tmj.2020.0068

146 Griffiths, K. M., Farrer, L., & Christensen, H. (2010). The efficacy of internet interventions for depression and anxiety disorders: A review of randomised controlled trials. *The Medical Journal of Australia*, 192, S4–S11.

147 Hammond, G. C., Croudace, T. J., Radhakrishnan, M., Lafortune, L., Watson, A., McMillan-Shields, F., & Jones, P. B. (2012). Comparative effectiveness of cognitive therapies delivered face-to-face or over the telephone: An observational study using propensity methods. *PLoS ONE*, 7(9), 1–15. https://doi.org/10.1371/journal.pone.0042916

148 Di Carlo, F., Sociali, A., Picutti, E., Pettorruso, M., Vellante, F., Verrastr, V., … & di Giannantonio, M. (2020). Telepsychiatry and other cutting-edge technologies in COVID-19 pandemic: Bridging the distance in mental health assistance. *The International Journal of Clinical Practice*, 75(1), 1–9. https://doi.org/10.1111/ijcp.13716

149 Bashshur, R. L., Doarn, C. R., Frenk, J. M., Kvedar, J. C., Shannon, G., W., & Woolliscroft, J. O. (2020). Beyond the COVID pandemic, telemedicine, and health care. *Telemedicine and e-Health*, 26(11), 1310–1313. https://doi.org/10.1089/tmj.2020.0328

150 Cieślik, B., Mazurek, J., Rutkowski, S., Kiper, P., Turolla, A., & Szczepańska-Gieracha, J. (2020). Virtual reality in psychiatric disorders: A systematic review of reviews. *Complementary Therapies in Medicine*, 52(2), 1–15. https://doi.org/10.1016/j.ctim.2020.102480

151 Shiban, Y., Fruth. M. B., Pauli, P., Kinateder, M., Reichenberger, J., & Mühlberger, A. (2016). Treatment effect on biases in size estimation in spider phobia. *Biological Psychology*, 121(Part B), 146–152. https://doi.org/10.1016/j.biopsycho.2016.03.005

152 Opriş, D., Pintea, S., García-Palacios, A., Botella, C., Szamosközi, Ş., & David, D. (2012). Virtual reality exposure therapy in anxiety disorders: a quantitative meta-analysis. *Depression and Anxiety*, 29(2), 85–93.

153 Roepke, A. M., Jaffee, S. R., Riffle, O. M., McGonigal, J., Broome, R., & Maxwell, B. (2015). Randomized controlled trial of SuperBetter, a smartphone-based/Internet-based self-help tool to reduce depressive symptoms. *Games for Health Journal*, 4, 235–246.

154 Marshall, J. M., Dunstan, D. A., & Bartik, W. (2020). Treating psychological trauma in the midst of COVID-19: The role of smartphone apps. *Frontiers in Public Health*, 8, 1–5. https://doi.org/10.3389/fpubh.2020.00402

155 Schueller, S. M., & Torous, J. (2020). Scaling evidence-based treatments through digital mental health. *American Psychologist*, 75(8), 1093–1114. https://doi.org/10.1037/amp0000654

156 Schueller & Torous (2020), 1093–1104.

157 Markowitz, J. C., & Milrod, B. L. (2015). What to do when a psychotherapy fails. *The Lancet Psychiatry*, 2(2), 186–190.

158 Markowitz & Milrod (2015).

159 Markowitz & Milrod (2015).

160 World Health Organization. (2016). *Suicide data*. www.who.int/mental_health/prevention/suicide/suicideprevent/en/

161 World Health Organization. (2019, 9 September). *Suicide in the world. Global health estimates*. www.who.int/publications/i/item/suicide-in-the-world

162 Hedegaard, H., Curtin, S. C., & Warner, M. (2020, April). *Increase in suicide mortality in the United States, 1999–2018*. National Center for Health Statistics. www.cdc.gov/nchs/products/databriefs/db330.htm

163 Olson, R. (n.d.). Centre for Suicide Prevention. www.suicideinfo.ca/resource/suicideandlanguage/

164 Curtin, S. C., & Hedegaard, H. (2019). *Suicide rates for females and males by race and ethnicity: United States, 1999 and 2017*. National Center for Health Statistics. www.cdc.gov/nchs/data/hestat/suicide/rates_1999_2017.htm

165 Centers for Disease Control and Prevention. (2015). *Suicide*. www.cdc.gov/violenceprevention/pdf/suicide-datasheet-a.PDF

166 Johns, M. M., Lowry, R., Haderxhanaj, L. T., Rasberry, C. N., Robin, L., Scales, L., … & Suarez, N. A. (2020). *Morbidity and mortality weekly report supplements*. www.cdc.gov/mmwr/volumes/69/su/su6901a3.htm?s_cid=su6901a3_x

167 Gonzales, G., Loret de Mola, E., Gavulic, K. A., McKay, T., & Purcell, C. (2020). Mental health needs among lesbian, gay, bisexual, and transgender college students during the COVID-19 pandemic. *Journal of Adolescent Health, 67*(5), 645–648. https://doi.org/10.1016/j.jadohealth.2020.08.006

168 Centers for Disease Control and Prevention. (2016). *Suicide: Risk and protective factors*. www.cdc.gov/ViolencePrevention/suicide/riskprotectivefactors.html

169 Centers for Disease Control and Prevention. (2016).

170 Seligman, M. E., & Csikszentmihalyi, M. (2014). *Positive psychology: An introduction* (pp. 279–298). Springer.

171 Khan, A., & Husain, A. (2010). Social support as a moderator of positive psychological strengths and subjective well-being. *Psychological Reports, 106*(2), 534–538.

172 Thoits, P. A. (2011). Mechanisms linking social ties and support to physical and mental health. *Journal of Health and Social Behavior, 52*(2), 145–161.

173 Marcussen, K. (2005). Explaining differences in mental health between married and cohabiting individuals. *Social Psychology Quarterly, 68*(3), 239–257.

174 King, L. A., Hicks, J. A., Krull, J. L., & Del Gaiso, A. K. (2006). Positive affect and the experience of meaning in life. *Journal of Personality and Social Psychology, 90*(1), 179–196.

175 Steger, M. F., & Dik, B. J. (2010). Work as meaning: Individual and organizational benefits of engaging in meaningful work. In P. A. Linley, S. Harrington, N. Garcea, P. A. Linley, S. Harrington, & N. Garcea (Eds.), *Oxford handbook of positive psychology and work* (pp. 131–142). Oxford University Press.

176 Grouden, M. E., & Jose, P. E. (2014). How do sources of meaning in life vary according to demographic factors? *New Zealand Journal of Psychology, 43*(3), 29–38.

177 Galek, K., Flannelly, K. J., Ellison, C. G., Silton, N. R., & Jankowski, K. B. (2015). Religion, meaning and purpose, and mental health. *Psychology of Religion and Spirituality, 7*(1), 1–12. https://doi.org/10.1037/a0037887

178 Heine, S. J., Proulx, T., & Vohs, K. D. (2006). The meaning maintenance model: On the coherence of social motivations. *Personality and Social Psychology Review, 10*(2), 88–110.

179 Biddle, S. J., & Mutrie, N. (2007). *Psychology of physical activity: Determinants, well-being and interventions*. Routledge.

180   Ahn, S., & Fedewa, A. L. (2011). A meta-analysis of the relationship between children's physical activity and mental health. *Journal of Pediatric Psychology*, 36(4), 385–397.

181   Biddle, S. J., & Mutrie, N. (2007). *Psychology of physical activity: Determinants, well-being and interventions*. Routledge.

182   Carmody, J., & Baer, R. A. (2008). Relationships between mindfulness practice and levels of mindfulness, medical and psychological symptoms and well-being in a mindfulness-based stress reduction program. *Journal of Behavioral Medicine*, 31(1), 23–33.

183   Sin, N. L., & Lyubomirsky, S. (2009). Enhancing well-being and alleviating depressive symptoms with positive psychology interventions: A practice-friendly meta-analysis. *Journal of Clinical Psychology*, 65(5), 467–487.

184   Goyal, M., Singh, S., Sibinga, E. M., Gould, N. F., Rowland-Seymour, A., Sharma, R., ... & Ranasinghe, P. D. (2014). Meditation programs for psychological stress and well-being: A systematic review and meta-analysis. *JAMA Internal Medicine*, 174(3), 357–368.

185   Barton, J., & Pretty, J. (2010). What is the best dose of nature and green exercise for improving mental health? A multi-study analysis. *Environmental Science & Technology*, 44(10), 3947–3955.

186   Barton & Pretty (2010).

187   Zoellner, T., & Maercker, A. (2006). Posttraumatic growth in clinical psychology – A critical review and introduction of a two component model. *Clinical Psychology Review*, 26(5), 626–653.

188   World Health Organization. (2003). *Mental health in emergencies*. http://apps.who.int/disasters/repo/8656.pdf

189   Calhoun, L. G., & Tedeschi, R. G. (2014). *Handbook of posttraumatic growth: Research and practice*. Routledge.

190   Blix, I., Birkeland, M. S., Hansen, M. B., & Heir, T. (2016). Posttraumatic growth – An antecedent and outcome of posttraumatic stress: Cross-lagged associations among individuals exposed to terrorism. *Clinical Psychological Science*, 4(4), 620–628.

Section 3   My wealth

Wealth can be defined and discussed from so many perspectives, and although money and monetary wealth are important (and presented in this section), here we more broadly present the concept of psychological wealth (and to be fair, we present other aspects of psychological wealth in other sections throughout this book). The late Ed Diener and his son, Robert Biswas-Diener[1], believed that psychological wealth consisted of the following ideas or components:

- life satisfaction and happiness
- spirituality and meaning in life
- positive attitudes and emotions
- loving social relationships
- engaging activities and work
- values and life goals to achieve them
- physical and mental health
- material sufficiency to meet our needs

As you will read, many of these concepts are presented here, and the remainder addressed throughout this book.

Part 3.1 Rich versus enriched – what's the difference?

Values in American life – our shared principles or behavioral standards – change only gradually, but they can change. These changes represent a bell-wether or what psychologists refer to as a predictor of new beliefs and behaviors. Consider these facts: A recent national survey of over 153,000 American high school students entering college found that over 67% agreed strongly or somewhat strongly that the chief benefit of a college education is that it increases a person's earning power.[2] Eighty-six percent of these students also claimed that to get a better job was a very important reason for going to college.[3] Not surprisingly, perhaps, almost 73% indicated that being able to make more money was an important reason for attending college, whereas just shy of 44% thought becoming a more cultured (i.e., educated or sophisticated) person was a good reason for pursuing higher education.[4] Compare these endorsements to past perspectives: Under 50% of college-bound students in a 1976 version of

DOI: 10.4324/9781003188711-4

the same survey viewed a college education as important because it offered a way "to be able to make more money."[5] What's going on? Why the change in values toward greater financial gain?

Students, like many of their fellow citizens, are now more focused on money matters (e.g., current earnings, potential salary, cost of living, loans, and debt) and materialism, the tendency to view possessions and comfort as more important than personal, spiritual, or social values. Certainly, the Great Recession, which most economists say occurred between 2007 and 2009, is one possible cause for the increased emphasis on money, as many Americans lost their jobs, savings, homes, and health insurance. The COVID-19 pandemic in 2020 and 2021 did not help economic matters, either, as many people became unemployed. But there are other potential causes. Our access to and reliance on media, whether traditional television, internet, or smart phones, introduces us to desirable toys and status symbols, such as the "right" clothing, car, sneakers, or smartwatch. And no doubt you can think of other reasons American culture has become more collectively acquisition-oriented and status seeking, and perhaps you recognize those moments in your own life where what you *want* overrides what you actually *need*.

Leading a satisfying and meaningful life is not only about money and material gains. We do need money and some possessions to survive, of course, but understanding how money affects happiness is an important issue. Let's begin by acknowledging that people's experienced sense of well-being (their feelings during moments of daily living) rises with income; in other words, higher incomes are aligned with feeling better day-to-day and feeling more satisfied with life overall.[6] Why? Well, perhaps higher incomes provide a greater sense of security? In fact, other researchers reported that higher incomes encourage people to evaluate their lives in more favorable terms. More to the point, though, higher incomes were found to be associated with more positive self-regarding emotions (like pride) and fewer negative self-regarding emotions (like anxiety).[7] Greater wealth leads people to feel prouder, as well as more confident and contented – and, simultaneously, less afraid, sad, and ashamed.

But, there is more to living life than focusing on the balance in one's bank account or retirement savings; in fact, too much focus on such items, as we shall see, can be counterproductive. To thrive in our daily lives, we need to be *enriched* rather than *rich*. To become enriched, we need to act to improve or enhance the quality of our lives by the relationships we form and maintain, the activities we choose to do in our spare time, the work we elect to pursue, and so on. In this section of the book, we explore how to live an enriched life where wealth is considered broadly by our emotions, our choices, and how we spend our time and money.

Part 3.2 Having money or not: Why does it matter?

Does money make your world go around? Should it? To be sure, having access to money to cover our bills and expenses does make life go more smoothly. Worrying about money or having too little of it is not pleasant and, in fact, can be quite stressful. Yet it turns out that our relationship with money is more complex than covering our debts, buying food, or exchanging bills and coins for various goods and services. As we will see, there are good and bad sides to our focus on money.

Costs associated with money fixation. Open your wallet, purse, billfold, or money clip. Take out whatever bills you have and hold them in your hand. Take a good look at your money. What images does it bring to mind? How does it make you feel?

Ultimately, money is symbolic, – as it represents something else, including options and possibilities. That colored, engraved paper bill you are holding is just that – a piece of *paper*. The coins clinking in your pocket or change purse are nothing but bits of common metal with little actual worth. The real or inherent value of money is little or nothing until cultures, nations, banks, and governments attach meaning to it. The concept and shared understanding of money enables us to exchange it for goods or services, which makes it a portable *tool* of sorts that literally affords us the opportunity to get items (whether physical or experiential) we need or want.

Yet not everyone uses the money they have; some people save it for a rainy day and still others hoard it. Why hold on to a tool (and a flimsy paper one at that) that isn't used? This quality has encouraged some researchers to characterize money as a sort of *drug* as well as a tool, in that humans want to possess it and hold on to more and more of it.[8]

Why a drug? Many drugs give us illusory and short-lived jolts of pleasure (i.e., until we ingest more of the drug to keep the buzz going), so we begin to want (and often need, even crave) the drug for its own sake. The drug becomes addictive and, to a certain extent, wanting to acquire more and more money is like that, too. It becomes an addiction of acquisition; some people want more and more of it even if they don't spend it. The saving or hoarding of money becomes the motivation, not necessarily what it can do for them as a tool.

Fortunately, most of us don't hoard money, but we do think about money much of the time, probably daily or even several times a day. Regardless of where they live in the world, most people can't help doing so. What happens when people think about dollars, Euros, or the Yen? Psychologist Kathleen Vohs and her colleagues discovered that there are very clear psychological and social consequences associated with thinking about money.[9] College students were primed to think about money by either being exposed to it (real money or play Monopoly bills) or not. Just being exposed to something in passing makes it more accessible in memory but not necessarily in a conscious way. In fact, events[10] in our daily experience *prime* us all the time, subtly or not so subtly. If you are in a restaurant and someone says "hot," you may think of "dog" because of where you are, but if you were outside and heard that word you might think of "sun" or "weather." The money priming was accomplished in a variety of different ways, including having some students read an essay that mentioned money and having others simply count the bills in a stack of play money.

What happened? In general, the students in the various experiments who encountered the money primes became more self-sufficient and independent; they worked longer than control participants on various tasks and when asked to express a preference, they chose to work alone on an activity rather than contributing their efforts to a team. Well, being independent and self-sufficient are generally seen as positive qualities, especially in particular settings like classrooms and workplaces. Both these qualities also represent American values, as self-sufficiency and independence do lead to good things, like goal-setting and achievement. In other words, money has an instrumental value because it allows people to achieve goals without seeking assistance from others.[11,12]

Still, Vohs and colleagues observed that there are some social costs associated with money on the mind.[13] In one experiment, while completing a questionnaire, students sat in front of a computer and saw a screen saver with various currencies floating under water, fish swimming under water, or no screen saver. They were then told they would be having a "get acquainted conversation" with another student. The participant was then asked to move two chairs together while the experimenter left the room briefly to get the other student. The students primed by money placed the chairs farther apart from one another than did those who saw the fish screen saver or no screen saver. The upshot: People primed by money become less sociable by creating greater social distance between themselves and potential new friends than those who aren't thinking about money.[14]

Nonverbal cues like social distance represent powerful behavioral choices that send a message. How many times have you picked up on a vibe that a stranger you encounter (say, someone sitting next to you on an airplane or a bus) wants to remain that way? Or, how often have you "shut down" friendly overtures from others without saying a word (e.g., burying your nose in a book, listening to your MP3 player oblivious to your surroundings, not meeting another person's gaze). The point in Voh's study is that the participants were oblivious to the fact that merely thinking about money made them act in ways less open to making a new acquaintance.

In another experiment, the investigators expected that a money prime would make people less helpful.[15] They were right. All students first played the classic board game Monopoly with a confederate (ostensibly a fellow student but really an aide to the experimenter) for several minutes. Students in a "high money" condition had $4,000 in Monopoly money (which is a lot if you are familiar with the game) while those in the "low money" group had just $200 (the students in the control condition had no play money left). Students in the two money conditions could see their money during the next stage of the experiment, where some were asked to imagine a wealthy future ("high money" group), a constrained financial future ("low money" group), or to reflect on their plans for the next day. A staged pratfall then occurred when a second confederate (who was unaware to which condition the student participant was assigned) appeared. While walking past the student, the confederate spilled a box of 27 pencils right in front of him or her. Those students in the high money group picked up fewer pencils (an average of 18) – and hence were less helpful – than those in the low money or control group, who picked up more or less the same number (about 20 pencils). The researchers suggested that being focused on wealth or riches makes people less helpful to others in need, even when the need is happening right in front of them.

But wait, what if we have money readily available to us, as when we have an unexpected windfall (e.g., we find $10 on the sidewalk, grandmother sends us a birthday check, we receive a tax rebate from the IRS)? Shouldn't we be more charitable or generous toward others? Alas, not if we are primed to think about the money.[16] In this experiment, student participants were given $2 in quarters for taking part in the research (little did they know receiving the quarters ensured they would have some money to later donate). The students then unscrambled some 15 sentences of five jumbled words into meaningful sentences of four words. Half of the students unscrambled sentences that were related to money ("high a salary desk paying" for "a high paying salary" – the fifth word, "desk," wasn't used to construct the sentence) and the other half did the same with sentences unrelated to money ("cold it desk outside is" for "it is cold outside" – again, in this example, "desk" was dropped). All the students then completed some filler questionnaires and were debriefed by the experimenter (informed about the study's supposed purpose although the actual experiment wasn't yet over). As she casually left the room, the experimenter mentioned that the lab was accepting donations for the "University Student Fund" and that there was a donation box next to the exit door if the student wished to donate. As you probably guessed, the students who were primed by money (via the four-word sentences) made much lower donations to the fund (an average of 77 cents) than those who were not thinking about money (an average of $1.34). Students who weren't thinking about the money gave almost double the donation compared to those who did.

This last study has connections to everyday life, as many times, especially around holidays, checkout clerks often ask patrons if they would like to "make a donation to feed the hungry" or to "help the homeless" by adding additional money to their receipt. When we are making a purchase in the grocery line, for example, money is naturally on our minds because we are whipping out our debit card, writing a check, or taking out cash to complete the purchase. At the same time we feel some pressure to make a donation (it can be hard to look cheap when a salesperson asks you to help the needy, whether they are people living on the street or pets in a shelter), we may end up giving less because the combination of paying the bill and hearing the cash register drawer open (not to mention parting with real or digital cash or credit) has put us in a money mind. Perhaps it would be better to ask for such donations before we make our way through the checkout line?

So, we now know that focusing on money doesn't necessarily promote happiness – or at least the sort of happiness that is linked with prosocial behaviors, such as donating to charity, getting to know new people, or offering help. But what factors are associated with our happiness and well-being? And can money buy us some happiness?

Part 3.3 Can money buy happiness?

Although our happiness is not necessarily predicated on money, some psychologists suggest that earnings *per se* are not the issue; it's not how much income we make, rather, it's how we choose to spend our money that matters. These researchers argue that there are actually particular ways we should go about spending our money in order to promote our own well-being or that of others. In this section, we will consider how best to spend money on ourselves and then on others, but before we do that, we will consider the importance of buying time for ourselves.

Time isn't money. One cultural cliché (usually attributed to Benjamin Franklin) states that "time is money," meaning, for example, if you are not using your time wisely, then you are essentially losing money. There is ample evidence indicating that as incomes rise, discretionary or leisure time gets reduced. How should we think about time and money?

Social psychologist Elizabeth Dunn (no relation to this book's co-author) and marketing professor Michael Norton argue that the problem is that people with higher incomes spend much of their days performing activities that make them feel stressed and tense, such as commuting to the office, working, doing housework, and shopping.[17,18,19,20] We want more time to do those tasks we find pleasant, like reading a good book, going for long and leisurely walk in the park, going to the museum, a concert, or a play, and so on. But instead, we find ourselves doing tasks that are not pleasant, which alters our moods and outlooks. Perhaps, argue Dunn and Norton, there are ways we can learn to "buy time" to deal with some disagreeable tasks in order to replace them with more fun ones.

In the first place, why should valuing time over money matter? Researchers revealed that people who routinely prioritize their time over money invest more time in meaningful social connections and interactions with other people.[21] In one of the studies, people who valued their time socialized longer with a new friend than those who valued their money. These social connection results were not explained by personality (extraversion) or any demographic qualities (gender, age, or income level). In another study, experimenters found that research participants who construed time as a scarce commodity (they imagined they were living their last month in their current city) reported higher levels of well-being across time than did a control group.[22]

Another relevant question is this one: What might be some good ways to spend money to obtain more time? Well, if there are particular chores that you especially dislike, such as cleaning your apartment, cutting the lawn, or doing laundry, then paying someone else, either a person or a service, to do some of these things might not be bad investment. (Of course, if you enjoy some of these activities – perhaps you find ironing to be relaxing and mowing the lawn to be a good time to think – then you shouldn't give them up.) Researchers posited that reminding people that they may be very busy in their futures prompted them to "buy time" by engaging services to do the necessary work.[23] The good news is that when people have more free time available for themselves, they often use it to do volunteer work, to get physical exercise, or to take part in other activities that enhance their happiness.[24] Outsourcing some responsibilities can reduce our sense of time pressure and allow us to redirect our focus from responsibilities to pleasure and play.

It turns out that just thinking about time rather than money has some benefits. One experiment required participants to do a simple puzzle task that primed them to think about time or money.[25] Half of them were given sentences to unscramble that got them to think about time (e.g., "sheets change the clock" could be rewritten as "change the clock" or "change the sheets"). The remaining participants deciphered sentences that encouraged them to think about money (e.g., "sheets change the price" could be "change the price" or "change the sheets"). Following the unscrambling task, all participants were asked to determine how to spend the next day. Those in the time-focused group were more likely to plan opportunities to socialize with other people or to spend quality time with a romantic partner rather than doing something work-related. In contrast, those in the money-focused group reported opposite choices: They intended to work rather than socialize or be with their lover. These surprising findings can probably be explained by the fact that time and money lead us to frame our thoughts quite differently.[26] Our choices about how we use our time appear to be directly linked to our sense of self, while our choices regarding money cause our thoughts to become somewhat cold, calculating, and rational.

One solution to the time versus money conundrum is to try to disassociate the two from one another as often as you can. We cannot stop thinking about money because we need it to survive and we frequently end up using it for purchases and to pay bills; however, we can try to stop thinking of time *as* money. Instead, we should view time as a worthy pursuit on its own. There are certainly lots of ways to spend time that can end up enriching our lives. To be sure, some of our choices will cost some money, such as taking up yoga or a painting or photography class, but it will be money well spent on an enriching activity.

Other items may not cost us that much but can repay us with higher levels of subjective well-being. For example, doing volunteer work even for a short period of time gives people the sense that they have more free time available in their daily lives.[27] Using our time to help others makes us feel like we have greater control over ourselves – if we can take the time to help others, then we must have our own lives in good working order.[28] Finally, sometimes giving away time to an activity, especially a routine one like walking the dog, can give us the sense that we have more time available.[29] Most dogs have to be walked daily (especially bigger ones), and what is assuredly a necessary responsibility can pay us back by providing regular exercise, just as it will get us to commune with the outdoors (there are emotional and cognitive advantages associated with connecting with nature, for example) while having passing conversations with friends, neighbors, and other dog walkers.[30] More exercise (within reasonable limits) leads to more happiness,[31] and where older adults are concerned, the presence of a dog will ensure they walk more than will a spouse or a friend.[32]

Although we can sometimes focus on time rather than money, the fact is that all of us must make spending decisions all of the time. Are there ways to spend our money a bit more strategically that can prove to be enriching?

Strategic spending for yourself. Let's assume you have a portion of your monthly budget set aside for personal expenses – which actually assumes you have a monthly budget. How should you spend it? Psychological researchers advance three approaches to what we call strategic spending on yourself that provide some psychosocial benefits: Buying experiences, enjoying a treat, and buying now only to consume later.

When people go on vacation, they often bring back trinkets, souvenirs, and other purchases that are meant to remind them of their travels. As you might guess, the magic associated with these material goods fades across time. – When we see our "Go Acapulco" t-shirt or that dress or tie we had to have from *Harrod's*, we may pause for a moment and briefly remember the pleasures associated with our trip. However, that pleasure is linked to the experience itself, not our clothing purchases. And there lies a real and basic recommendation for all of us to consider: Buy experiences rather than things.[33]

At the same time, we can all admit that some material things, – say, a gift from a loved one or a purchase we saved up for – can provide us with some happiness. In fact, research demonstrates that material purchases provide more **momentary happiness** – that is, enjoyment felt when the purchase is actually acquired – as compared to **experiential happiness** or pleasure tied to live events involving spending money, such as a dinner out or a weekend away from home. Across time, material purchases tend to provide more *frequent* momentary happiness whereas experiential purchases allow for more *intense* momentary happiness on distinct occasions.[34] (You will learn more about happiness later in Section 5.)

What do we mean by "experiences" besides meals, trips, and vacations? Well, almost anything that qualifies as a life experience, such as attending a concert by your favorite musician or band (Neil Young, Alabama Shakes, or Beyoncé, anyone?), enjoying a celebratory milestone (birthday, promotion, graduation, engagement), attending an exciting sporting event (a Red Sox game, the Super Bowl), going to an arts festival – the list is long and will vary from person to person due to individual interests, tastes, and opportunities. The point is that greater happiness is associated with buying experiences rather than things. In one study, researchers asked people to reflect on past purchases of tangible objects (furniture, jewelry, clothing, digital devices) or experiences like those we just mentioned.[35] When asked which made them happier, the majority chose the experiential purchases over the material ones.

What makes experiences more enjoyable than material goods (besides the fact that we inevitably adjust to the latter)? If you think about it, most of our experiences take place with other people involved. We may go on a trip with family, dine out with friends, celebrate a birthday with both friends and family, and so on. Other people make the experience more enjoyable because they share in it and benefit from it, too. So, experiences make us feel connected to others, while most material purchases are linked mostly to the self.[36] Isn't running a 5K more fun because there are other people running with you? Aren't summer blockbuster movies enjoyable precisely because the audience in the theater reacts as one to the rampaging dinosaurs, cascading floodwaters, or adorable computer-generated characters? It turns out, too, that experiential purchases are seen as playing a greater role in our life narratives and sense of self than do material purchases.[37] Thus, despite our reliance (really, staggering dependence) on our smart phones, they don't mean as much as when it comes to defining ourselves as that trip to the Grand Canyon or to Vienna, Austria. And here's a real kicker about the power of experiences: Even bad ones (the trip to Maine where it rained the entire week, the beachfront hotel with terrible food and intermittent air conditioning) become more pleasant in our memories.[38,39] We can laugh about them in retrospect, as they are also part of ourselves and can make an entertaining story.

A second approach to self-spending entails a bit of self-control. All of us spend money on items we enjoy – and many of us do so frequently. These items need not be big purchases. Perhaps you need a pick-me-up most afternoons so you buy a chocolate bar from the vending machine in the building where you work. Or, when you start each day's commute, you pull into the local *Starbucks* and get the vanilla chai latte for the drive. Over a long weekend, you might camp out in the family room to binge watch several seasons of a TV series on Netflix. Is there any downside here? As you may have already guessed, we get used to the things in our life, so that the more we have them, the less we truly appreciate them (Thursday's chai was a little less delightful than Monday's, the 30th episode of *Breaking Bad* has less novelty and pleasure associated with it than the ones viewed earlier).[40]

A good way to cope with our inevitable hedonic adjustment to whatever things we enjoy buying is to turn them into treats.[41] By "treat," the object of desire remains a desire much of the time – instead of having it every day, we parcel out our pleasure so that we have it on occasion. Chocolate will remain a rich treat if we eat it once or twice a week rather than daily (and just think of the saved calories), as will whatever complicated coffee beverage we indulge in. Note that you are not eliminating your consumption and enjoyment of whatever it is you enjoy; rather, you are altering the pattern of consumption, allowing yourself to look forward to future pleasure rather than immediate or frequent gratification. Turning little pleasures into treats is one of the easiest spending habits you can develop, and it is one that is likely to provide you with a genuine source of pleasure.[42] Why not give it a try?

The third self-spending strategy will probably seem a little odd to many readers, as it is a twist on delaying pleasure. The recommendation is that we should pay in advance for whatever we want but postpone consuming it until a future time. That's right, pay now, enjoy later. This suggestion is at odds with American culture where credit cards promote the reverse process, allowing us to consume now and pay later. (And many people end up overspending in the joyful moment only to be floored by the bill appearing on their next credit card statement.)

It turns out that there is ample evidence that postponing pleasure actually makes it more enjoyable. Researchers, for example, found that would-be vacationers enjoyed higher levels of happiness as they anticipated the joys of their trip in the weeks before they took it – and they also reported higher levels of happiness before the trip as compared to after it.[43] Similarly, think how often you anticipate future pleasures, such as the party you will attend a week from now, a break from work next month, or the holiday rush that occurs in the corridor from Thanksgiving to New Year's day (and isn't the month of January usually a big letdown?).

But how do we pay ahead? You can order something in advance, before it is released, for example, or you can buy an item online and enjoy the wait as it wends its way through the mail system to your home. Waiting a few days or a week or even longer for whatever it is to arrive is apt to give you more pleasure (you anticipate how you will feel when it comes) than will heading to the mall and buying it right now would give you. By this logic, as odd as it might seem, we might get more pleasure out of paying for a new CD in advance and waiting for it to be mailed to us instead of downloading the whole album immediately onto our MP3 player or smart phone. Plain and simple, anticipating future pleasures feels good and serves as a reward of sorts.[44]

Obviously, not every purchase should be delayed. We need food to eat, just as we need to have fuel in our cars. And our routine bills (heat, electricity) must be paid. Necessary spending, then, generally is immune from the anticipated pleasure effect.[45] But some purchases should be postponed, as when we receive a gift card for our favorite store or restaurant. It's probably better to think about what you will buy with the gift card (that new bestselling novel, your favorite gooey pasta dish) for a while than it is to run right out and make the purchase.

Our final recommendation concerning enriching strategic spending deals with spending money on other people rather than yourself, or **prosocial spending**.[46,47] The following experiment illustrates why spending money on others can enhance our happiness more than buying things for ourselves.[48] Passersby were approached and invited to take part in an experiment. If they agreed, they were asked to provide their phone number, report how happy they were at present, and were then given an envelope. Inside the envelope was a $5.00 bill and a note. Some participants received this note: "Please spend this $5.00 today before 5pm on a gift for yourself or any of your expenses (e.g., rent, bills, or debt)." Others read this note: "Please spend this $5.00 today before 5pm on a gift for someone else or a donation to charity." Still others received similar envelopes containing $20, not $5.

In the evening, all participants were phoned and asked how happy they felt and how they spent the money from the envelope.[49] Those who spent their windfall on themselves bought things like coffee, lunch, and earrings. Those who bought items for others treated friends to coffee, gave money to homeless persons, bought small presents for relatives, and so on. This prosocial spending ended up making the benefactors report higher levels of happiness than those who bought things for themselves, despite the fact that everyone started the day at the same level of self-reported happiness. And here is another surprising result of the study: – Whether they received $5 or $20 in the envelope made no difference in the levels of reported happiness, – as only the "spending on others" mattered. Indeed, related work found that giving money away to charity predicts greater levels of happiness in people than does spending money on themselves.[50] Prosocial spending is also linked to feelings of happiness in countries where incomes and standards of living are extremely low, even when spending on others may mean depriving oneself.[51]

Why does prosocial spending increase the happiness of those doing the spending? Doing things for others gives people feelings of warmth and connection, and this emotional influence has been observed from toddlers up to older adults.[52] Giving to or investing in other people seems to satisfy one or more human core needs, including competence, relatedness to others, and autonomy, and the psychosocial benefits of such prosocial spending have been tracked behaviorally as well as in the brain.[53] Even casual observers can tell that prosocial spending makes the buyer feel good.[54] When we help others by committing acts of even modest generosity, we are also helping ourselves and benefiting from our own actions.[55] Surprisingly, even giving away a modest amount of money, say $1, can actually make the donor feel wealthier as well as happier (recall the earlier research we discussed indicating that donating time led to a feeling of having more time – a feeling of having more money occurs when people give it away).[56] Knowing how to spend money can promote an enriched life – but so can flourishing, a topic we explore next.

Part 3.4 What does it mean to flourish?

What does it mean to flourish in daily life? How can flourishing be enriching? When people **flourish**, they enjoy high levels of psychological well-being and low levels of mental illness.[57,58] In contrast, people who are *struggling* experience high levels of both well-being and mental illness. A state known as **floundering** occurs if an individual displays high levels of mental illness and low levels of well-being. In turn, low levels of well-being and mental illness indicate an individual is *languishing*.[59]

Are flourishing in your life? Are you experiencing positive feelings regarding your personal relationships with friends and family? Are you optimistic about the future? Do you see purpose in what you do each day? Why not complete the scale shown in Table 3.1 to assess your level of flourishing?

What is your score on the Flourishing scale? If it is not as high as you expected or would like, don't despair – you now know there are things you can do to enrich your life and enhance your level of flourishing. And we will be learning about others in the pages that follow. In the meantime, keep in mind that flourishing is more than feeling joy or pleasure, or even recognizing and appreciating beauty. Flourishing is about believing that your actions – intentional and otherwise – serve a larger purpose and are highly engaging for you.[60]

Table 3.1 The flourishing scale[112]

Here are eight statements with which you may agree or disagree. Using the scale below, indicate your agreement with each item by indicating that response for each statement.

1	2	3	4	5	6	7
strongly disagree	disagree	slightly disagree	neither agree nor disagree	slightly agree	agree	strongly agree

1.____ I lead a purposeful and meaningful life
2.____ My social relationships are supportive and rewarding
3.____ I am engaged and interested in my daily activities
4.____ I actively contribute to the happiness and well-being of others
5. ____I am competent and capable in the activities that are important to me
6. ___ I am a good person and live a good life
7. ____I am optimistic about my future
8.____ People respect me

Scoring: Add the responses, varying from 1 to 7, for all eight items. Add your scores for these items on the scale and place your answer here: _____. Possible scores range from 8 to 56. A high score represents a person with many psychological resources and strengths.

What is the relationship or, rather, the *non*relationship between materialism and flourishing? Take a moment and consider how you would define the "American Dream." If you are like most people, being rich, having an expensive car, and living in a grand and enviable home likely come to mind. Being attractive and perhaps famous often end up on the list, too. Now, there is nothing wrong with having high aspirations for your future. Doing so allows you to set goals for yourself and to work toward meeting them. Problems occur, however, when our goals become overly focused on seeking financial success, social recognition, and possessing a pleasing appearance.[61,62] In fact, doing so is associated with higher levels of physical distress, lower self-actualization (self-actualization is the idea of living up to and meeting one's own potential), and reduced energy and liveliness. Instead, being focused on self-acceptance, having helpful feelings for one's community, desiring to affiliate with others, and pursuing physical fitness predict healthy mental and physical well-being. Seeking intrinsic values that lead to intimacy, individual growth, and contribute to the wider good leads to an enriched life, whereas a focus on extrinsic, materialistic goals does not.[63]

Undue focus on materialism, then, can be tiring and – as one psychologist put it – "toxic for happiness."[64] Social psychologist Tim Kasser agrees, as he demonstrated that the desire for material gain creates a frantic drive for acquiring things (including money, which we know facilitates buying things), one that means people must work hard to keep pace with their desires.[65] Unfortunately, getting what we want is usually accompanied by only a short-lived emotional "buzz," as new wants emerge, which means we want to switch focus and begin pursuit of the next shiny, new item. (Ask yourself honestly: How often have you wanted to upgrade to the newest smart phone, despite the fact that you probably don't use all of your current phone's capabilities?) And more stuff, whether it's clothing or technology or whatever, becomes just that – more stuff we must attend to that quickly loses luster and becomes absorbed (if not lost) among all of our other material possessions.

You might wonder why we quickly lose interest and enthusiasm in the things we "must have" once we have them. One compelling explanation is called the **hedonic treadmill theory**, where we eventually, often rather quickly, adjust to whatever good thing comes our way.[66,67] We desire it, work for it, obtain it, enjoy brief pleasure with it, and then it becomes, inexorably, just one more thing we own. (How many articles of clothing did you "have to have" but then wore only a few times? How many of them are still in bags or still have their price tags, the joy of the "get" having gone long before you ever put it on?) The term "treadmill" refers to generated activity that actually keeps us in the same place, like running on a treadmill for exercise in the gym. In terms of personal flourishing, we don't get anywhere because our feelings for whatever object seemed essential and wonderful gradually fades to a faint sense of pleasure. In effect, our happiness level spikes when we obtain whatever we sought (say, we go from a 6 to 7.5 on our imagined scale of happiness) and then we psychologically adjust to having our material triumph, usually close to where we were before (we drop back to 6 or thereabouts once more).

Perhaps one of the worst aspects of the treadmill theory is that there will always be another trinket, bauble, or big-ticket item we want. If our income level rises, we will want a costlier car, a bigger house, a longer and more elaborate vacation, a trendy new watch or camera, and so on. And we will go for it and if we obtain it, adjust to it, just like all the previous times. Where our happiness and flourishing are concerned, we don't seem to learn from our own past choices and actions, that desire fades once a goal or acquisition is achieved. Worse still, if our income doesn't rise, we will work that much harder to increase our earning power, sapping our energy and positive outlook in the process, so that the objects of our desire can be had sooner rather than later.

Is there any good news about our adjustment to material items? Well, yes, if you consider the consequences of bad items. People often think that negative events – such as accidents, unrealized promotions or raises, missed opportunities, lost jobs, and the like – will wreck or undo their lives. Although not pleasant in the least, many people do adjust to the bad things that inevitably touch all our lives.[68] Beyond that, we are poor judges of predicting how we will feel in the future about good or bad events; we neglect to remember that such events occur among other life events, so that their positive or negative qualities have less than expected impacts on how we end up feeling.[69,70] Only some of the worst negative events (e.g., divorce, a serious and chronic health condition, long-term unemployment, death of a partner) appear to create a seismic change in our subjective well-being, so that our sense of happiness is changed in a downward direction for some time, even permanently.[71,72,73]

Kasser's work also reveals that materialist tendencies often emerge from feelings of deep personal insecurity.[74] The desire of wanting to have more things is typically found among people who feel less competent and in control of their lives than others, who are unsure about romance and love, and who lack robust self-esteem. Shopping and buying items seem like a way to fill the void or feelings of emptiness. After all, if we can't develop self-esteem or a sense of accomplishment by who we are and what we do, then why not go after it by acquiring items that we hope will attract others' attention and admiration? Regrettably, our larger culture reinforces these views by what it values, such as celebrity, wealth, status symbols, youth, and other qualities associated with advertising and social media. So, being rich in money or objects does not lead to happiness or flourishing, nor is it a way to become enriched. We now turn to ways of becoming psychologically enriched.

Part 3.5 How can I increase my own enrichment?

What qualities make for a good and enriched life? Psychological researchers suggest that finding ways to experience positive emotions can make favorable contributions to our well-being. Let's begin with the importance of feeling good.

Positive emotions: Good for us. Until recently, psychologists knew much more about negative emotions than positive ones. One possible reason is that negative emotions, including anger, fear, guilt, and sadness, serve a warning or protective function for us. When we are worried or threatened, these unpleasant responses spur us to vigilance (*What's the danger?*) and specific action (*How do I get out of harm's way?*). Negative emotions also outnumber positive emotions about three to one;[75] in many respects, bad threats loom larger in our outlooks than good ones.[76] Fortunately, there has been a sea change lately in the study of emotion, so that psychologists are now very interested in the role positive emotions play in daily life and how we benefit from them.

Barbara Fredrickson developed the **broaden-and-build model** of positive emotions to explain these benefits.[77] Unlike their negative counterparts that narrow our focus, positive emotions open us up to a variety of behavioral options that can both promote and maintain our well-being. When people experience positive emotions, such as joy, happiness, gratitude, or contentment, they are apt to seek out social exchanges with others, aid people in need, try out new experiences, or engage in creative activities.[78,79]

In one experiment, for example, a group of people watched some film clips designed to trigger one of five emotions (joy, contentment, anger, fear, or a neutral condition).[80] The group members then generated written lists of everything they would like to have been doing at that moment in time. The individuals who experienced either joy or contentment listed more possible, desirable activities than those in either the negative or neutral emotion groups. Experiencing positive emotions apparently leads people to think more expansively, to consider many future things they might do, whereas negative and neutral emotions limit the scope of thoughts, thereby reducing the range of potential future actions. In effect, then, positive emotions broaden our outlooks while at the same time they allow us to develop personal resources (emotional as well as intellectual) to draw from in the future.[81]

On the basis of Fredrickson's research, we can conclude that positive emotions possess another beneficial quality, which she refers to as the **undoing hypothesis**.[82] When we experience positive emotions following negative ones, our good feelings aid both our minds and our bodies by returning us to a sense of balance and flexibility. Quite simply, positive emotions undo the aftereffects of negative feelings more quickly than would occur if those feelings remained negative or even neutral. When something bad happens (e.g., we witness a car accident for instance), the negative feelings associated with the event dissipate faster if we have a chance to discuss what we saw and how we felt with other witnesses. Sharing our shock and anxiety with others and recognizing that they felt the same way – thereby sharing the positive feelings of "we are in this together" – can eliminate any lingering stress.

Good feelings have good consequences for us. They give us a wider perspective on our situation and encourage us to connect with others in a variety of ways. So far, we've discussed positive emotions as responses to our experiences. In order to harness their power to enrich our lives, we need to consider how to generate our own positive emotions by developing particular qualities linked to them.

Part 3.6 How else can I enrich my everyday life?

To enrich your daily life, you may wish to cultivate some beneficial qualities, which are linked to performing particular intentional actions. We will consider three of them: Expressing gratitude, capitalizing on others' good fortune, and savoring our experiences.

Gratitude refers to the basic quality of being thankful and showing sincere appreciation for kind things that others do for us.[83] Gracious people are also able to return such kindness in the future, which means that gratitude can motivate self-improvement and other positive changes.[84] Psychologically, being able to express gratitude to others is beneficial because it enhances our social connectedness with them, just as it extends positive emotions (we feel good about what was done for us and for being able to express thanks, which, in turn, makes the other person feel good).[85] Being grateful also slows down our adjustment to good things – we stay beyond our happiness baseline a bit longer than usual. Other researchers indicate that feeling gratitude motivates us to want to give back to others and though the direction usually may be toward our benefactor, it need not be; we can give back more broadly than that.[86] One relatively easy way, then, to promote, share, and benefit from positive emotions is to express gratitude to the people in your life who do things great and small for you.

Of course, expressing gratitude does not have to be aimed at another person or persons literally; you can simply recall acts of kindness from the past[87] or just count your blessings by reflecting on the positive aspects of your life. In fact, doing so has benefits. Three intervention experiments had people engage in self-directed "count your blessings" sessions, either weekly for over two months or daily for a few weeks.[88] When compared to people in control groups, who spent their time reflecting on either negative or routine events during the same time periods, those in the gratitude groups not only reported higher levels of positive emotion, they also displayed better physical well-being. So, taking the time ask yourself, "What are the things in my life I am grateful for?" or "In what ways I am better off than other people?" on a regular basis may well pay dividends where good feelings and health are concerned.[89] As the late psychologist Chris Peterson put it, "Counting your blessings … makes you happier and more content with life."[90]

Besides expressing thanks for good things that happen to us, we should also attend to and celebrate the good things that happen to other people. **Capitalization** is a form of social support where positive events are shared with other people who express genuine interest or even joy in hearing them.[91] The way we share and react to good news can have psychological benefits for us as well as other people.[92] When we tell our romantic partner or a close friend about something good that happened to us (e.g., a promotion at work, a high grade on a school paper, a compliment from our supervisor), if our listener responds with interest and enthusiasm ("That's amazing! Good for you! You earned it!"), capitalization may result. Specifically, positive responses to a story or event elicits positive emotions in the sharer, which leads to mutual respect, appreciation, and a better, closer relationship.

An important point is that we, too, have to capitalize on the good things our friends and loved ones share with us. We need to listen with care, just as we need to respond with warmth and pleasure in the other's success. If we appear to be distracted or disinterested or even just plain bored ("Huh? What? Oh, really … I guess that's nice … it is nice, isn't it?"), then capitalization won't occur. Although we may not offend the other person, we certainly reduce the chances that he or she will share future happy events with us (who wants a "downer" response?) or bother to capitalize on whatever next good thing we share. Clearly, sometimes it is a challenge to listen to others' good news, especially if we are tired after a long day. We need to keep in mind, though, that if we want our own successes to be celebrated, then we have to respond well to those things our peers share with us.

Both capitalizing and expressing gratitude are actions that benefit the doer and the recipient. Let's consider a quality that is largely self-focused: **Savoring**. When we *savor*, we try to enhance the pleasure associated with some experience, whether it's a special moment (graduating from college) or a relatively routine one (lounging on the patio on a summer afternoon).[93] Savoring involves reflecting on the moment or moments linked to some event – we focus on the journey rather than the proverbial destination. This "process, not product" approach allows people to live in the moment by savoring a sunrise or sunset, a sweet-tart glass of lemonade on a hot summer's day, a pleasurable brunch with an old friend, a leisurely walk through a lovely garden, or a piece of familiar music (think classic rock) that reminds us of joyous times in the past.

The challenging part of savoring is that most of us describe ourselves as very busy, if not overcommitted, and we are usually pulled in different directions by what we need to do (responsibilities) and what we would prefer to do (desires).

Table 3.2 Qualities affecting the intensity of savoring events[113]

Duration. Setting aside dedicated time improves our chances of savoring an experience.

Stress reduction. Savoring is more likely to occur if we can distract ourselves from pressing, yet often somewhat stressful, concerns of everyday living (e.g., homework, chores to be done, answering emails).

Complexity. Complex experiences – looking at a complex painting, listening to a rich symphony, reading an absorbing novel – can deepen our savoring experiences.

Social connection. Savoring sounds as if it's a solo effort but often it's best when shared with others. Looking at a rainbow or enjoying an outdoor concert is much more satisfying when others are present to share the experience.

Balanced self-monitoring. Trying too hard or thinking too much can disrupt the ease with which we savor something. Savoring should be natural, not forced – it's not like a duty.

As you might expect, being focused on money, for example (thinking about it too much or too often) leads people to savor special moments less.[94] Too few of us take a regular opportunity to slow down in order to really reflect on what we are feeling, thinking, and doing. Savoring represents a thoughtful pause in time, one that goes beyond mere enjoyment of the activity. Five key qualities that affect the intensity of savored events are shown in Table 3.2.

Savoring actually adds clarity and vividness to people's experiences, thereby contributing to their happiness and well-being.[95] Nor is savoring difficult to do – with little trouble, it can make us feel more relaxed[96] while reducing negative emotions and the possibility of depressive symptoms.[97] How often do you savor the moment? To find out, complete the scale shown in Table 3.3.

What was your score on the savoring scale? As you can see, anyone can savor something, but the real issue is whether we remember the virtues and benefits of relishing a special moment. Can you remember the last time you truly savored an experience or an event? When will you have your next opportunity to savor an experience? Try to savor something later on today.

Part 3.7 Perhaps your best investment: You! (and why this is meaningful)

This section of the book demonstrates that there are concrete behaviors we can perform to enrich our lives and that money, while necessary, should not be the primary focus driving our choices. Moreover, the choices we make can also benefit other people, those we know and love, and many we've never met, as when we decide to donate to a charity or volunteer our time. Again, we do not need to be rich in order to become enriched. Initiating a few changes in your life based on the research evidence linked to this theme can pay decided psychosocial dividends where your happiness and well-being are concerned. The opportunity to flourish in daily living increases when you avoid the traps

Table 3.3 The savoring scale[114]

Assess each question by selecting the number that best describes your response. To what degree do you savor the present moment?

1. When good things have happened in your life, how much do you feel you have typically been able to appreciate or enjoy them?
1 = not at all 2 = a little bit 3 = some 4 = a lot 5 = a great deal

2. Compared to most other people you know, how much pleasure have you typically gotten from good things that have happened to you?
1 = none 2 = a little bit 3 = some 4 = a lot 5 = a great deal

3. When something good happens to you, compared to most other people you know, how long does it usually affect the way you feel? Provide a number ranging from 1 (not for very long) to 7 (for a very long time): _____

4. When good things have happened to you, have there ever been times when you felt like everything was really going your way; that is, when you felt on top of the world, or felt a great deal of joy in life, or found it hard to contain your positive feelings? How often would you say you felt like that?
1 = many times 2 = sometimes 3 = once in a while 4 = never

5. How often would you say that you feel like jumping for joy?
1 = never 2 = rarely 3 = sometimes 4 = often

Reverse the number you gave to question 4 (i.e., 1 = 4, 2 = 3, 3 = 2, 4 = 1) and then total your numbers for the five items. Scores can range from 5 to 25, with higher scores reflecting greater savoring of positive outcomes. Undergraduates in an introductory psychology course scored a mean of 18.76.

and trappings of materialism. Table 3.4 summarizes the main points regarding ways to live an enriched life.

Part 3.8 Putting it all together: Life is meaningful

We want to close this section by introducing an idea that ties together all of the enrichment activities: Recognizing that life is meaningful. Human beings are sense makers in that they look for and find meaning in experiences, events, and the lives of others. So, we know people readily find or make meaning all the time, but do they see their own lives as meaningful? Meaning in life can be defined in any number of ways, but three qualities are usually present:[98]

- A meaningful life is one with a sense of purpose.
- A meaningful life is one that matters or possesses some significance.

These qualities represent motivations, so their presence encourages people to behave in ways that are goal directed. What about the third quality?

- A meaningful life makes sense to the individual, who sees his or her experience in the world as predictable and marked by regularity.

Table 3.4 Ways to enrich your life: A summary list

Look beyond money – don't fixate on it – and appreciate what you have.
Remember that we quickly adjust to any new purchase, so that what we "had to have"
    soon becomes just another object or acquisition that loses its material potency.
Cultivate beneficial qualities (e.g., express gratitude to others, capitalize on others'
    good news, savor events) that increase your positive emotions.
Spend your money well by buying time and experiences, treating yourself on occasion,
    and paying ahead so you can enjoy later.
Perform prosocial spending on other people in order to help them and yourself.
Remember that life is meaningful.

This third quality is more cognitive than motivational, and it is based on how people reflect on and construe their own lives.

What about you? Do you see your life as meaningful? Find out by taking a few minutes now to complete the questionnaire found in Table 3.5.

Chances are good that you see your life as quite meaningful. Our lives are probably pretty meaningful because such belief is associated with a variety of positive qualities or outcomes.[99] Bear in mind that these associations are largely correlational, not causal. Still, their degree of consistency suggests that interesting and beneficial things are somehow linked with believing one has a meaningful life, including:

- Experiencing positive rather than negative moods.[100]
- Low incidence of psychological disorders.[101]
- Good quality of life[102] and self-reported health.[103]
- Slower age-related cognitive decline and lowered risk for Alzheimer's disease.[104]
- Low rates of loneliness or social exclusion.[105]
- Decreased mortality rates.[106]

Individuals who view their lives as meaningful tend to be better adjusted to the demand of their work and career lives than those who find less meaning.[107] People who rate their lives as meaningful are often seen as being more socially appealing to others than those who do not see their lives as meaningful.[108] And when challenges arise, as they inevitably will, people who see their lives as meaningful appear to deal with such obstacles by using adaptive coping strategies.[109]

Thus, the very good news is that a variety of studies reveal that seeing life as meaningful is widespread.[110] Rather than being something that is reserved for a chosen few, such as attractive, wealthy, or well-heeled individuals, most people appear to believe their lives are indeed significant. Belief in such meaning is adaptive, promoting our survival as humans.

We hope that you are like many of the participants in studies on meaning, whose thoughts, feelings, and actions indicate, "What I do has purpose. What I do has significance. My life matters in a way that will outlast my physical

Table 3.5 Meaning in life questionnaire (MLQ)[115]

Please take a moment to think about what in your life and existence feel important and significant to you. Please respond to the following statements as truthfully and accurately as you can, and also please remember that these are very subjective questions and that there are no right or wrong answers. Please answer according to the scale below:

1	2	3	4	5	6	7
absolutely untrue	mostly untrue	somewhat untrue	can't say true or false	somewhat true	mostly true	absolutely true

1. _____ I understand my life's meaning.
2. _____ I am looking for something that makes my life feel meaningful.
3. _____ I am always looking to find my life's purpose.
4. _____ My life has a clear sense of purpose.
5. _____ I have a good sense of what makes my life meaningful.
6. _____ I have discovered a satisfying life purpose.
7. _____ I am always searching for something that makes my life feel significant.
8. _____ I am seeking a purpose or mission for my life.
9. _____ My life has no clear purpose.
10. _____ I am searching for meaning in my life.

Scoring. The MLQ has two subscales, the Presence subscale and the Search Subscale. To determine your Presence score, add items 1, 4, 5, and 6, as well as item 9, which is reverse recoded (i.e., 1 = 7, 2 = 6, 3 = 5, 4 = 4, 5 = 3, 6 = 2, and 7 = 1). The Search score is determined by adding items 2, 3, 7, 8, and 10.

   Presence of Meaning score _____
   Search for Meaning score _____

The Presence of Meaning subscale measures how full respondents feel their lives are of meaning. The Search for Meaning subscale measures how engaged and motivated respondents are in efforts to find meaning or deepen their understanding of meaning in their lives. Presence is positively related to well-being, intrinsic religiosity, extraversion and agreeableness, and negatively related to anxiety and depression. Search is positively related to religious quest, rumination, past-negative and present-fatalistic time perspectives, negative affect, depression, and neuroticism, and negatively related to future time perspective, close-mindedness (i.e., dogmatism), and well-being. Presence is also related to personal growth self-appraisals, and altruistic and spiritual behaviors as assessed through daily diaries in relevant research.

existence."[111] Always remember, then, that life – your life – is meaningful. To be sure, that is an enriching thought.

Notes

1 Diener, E., & Biswas-Diener, R. (2008). *Happiness: Unlocking the mysteries of psychological wealth.* Blackwell Publishing.

2 Eagan, K., Stolzenberg, E. B., Ramirez, J. J., Aragon, M. C., Suchard, M., & Hurtado, S. (2014). *The American freshman: National norms for fall 2014* (p. 42). Higher Education Research Institute, UCLA.

3 Eagan et al. (2014), p. 43.

4 Eagan et al. (2014), p. 43.

5 Pryor, J. H., Hurtado, S. B., Saenz, V. B., Santos, J. L., & Korn, W. S. (2007). *The American freshman: Forty year trends* (p. 34). Higher Education Research Institute, UCLA.

6 Killingsworth, M. A. (2021). Experienced well-being rises with income, even above $75,000 per year. *Proceedings of the National Academy of Sciences, 118*(4). https://doi.org/10.1073/pnas.2016976118

7 Tong, E. M. W., Reddish, P., Oh, V. Y. S., Ng, W., Sasaki, E., Chin, E. D. A., & Diener, E. (2021). Income robustly predicts self-regard emotions. *Emotion.* https://doi.org/10.1037/emo0000933 (Supplemental).

8 Lea, S. E. G., & Webley, P. (2006). Money as tool, money as drug: The biological psychology of a strong incentive. *Behavioral and Brain Sciences, 29*(2), 161–209. https://doi.org/10.1017/S0140525X06009046

9 Vohs, K. D., Mead, N. L., & Goode, M. R. (2006). The psychological consequences of money. *Science, 314*(5802), 1154–1156. https://doi.org/10.1126/science.1132491

10 Bargh, J. A., & Chartrand, T. L. (2014). The mind in the middle: A practical guide to priming and automaticity research. In H. T. Reis & C. M. Judd (Eds.), *Handbook of research methods in social and personality psychology*, 2nd ed. (pp. 311–344). Cambridge University Press.

11 Lea, S. E. G., & Webley, P. (2006). Money as tool, money as drug: The biological psychology of a strong incentive. *Behavioral and Brain Sciences, 29*(2), 161–209. https://doi.org/10.1017/S0140525X06009046

12 Vohs, K. D., Mead, N. L., & Goode, M. R. (2006). The psychological consequences of money. *Science, 314*(5802), 1154–1156. https://doi.org/10.1126/science.1132491

13 Vohs et al. (2006).

14 Vohs et al. (2006), Experiment 7.

15 Vohs et al. (2006), Experiment 5.

16 Vohs et al. (2006), Experiment 6.

17 Dunn, E., & Norton, M. (2013). *Happy money: The science of happier spending.* Simon & Schuster.

18 Kahneman, D., Krueger, A. B., Schkade, D., Schwarz, N., & Stone, A. A. (2006). Would you be happier if you were richer? A focusing illusion. *Science, 312*(5728), 1908–1910. https://doi.org/10/1126/science.1129688

19 Whillans, A. V., Dunn, E. W., Smeets, P., Bekkers, R., & Norton, M. I. (2017). Buying time promotes happiness. *Proceedings of the National Academy of Sciences, 114*(32), 8523–8527. https://doi.org/10.1073/pnas.1706541114; www.pnas.org/cgi/doi/10.1073/pnas.1706541114

20 Dunn, E. W., Whillans, A. V., Norton, M. I., & Aknin, L. B. (2020). Prosocial spending and buying time: Money as a tool for increasing subjective well-being. In B. Gawronski (Ed.), *Advances in experimental social psychology* (Vol. 61, pp. 67–126). Elsevier.

21 Whillans, A. V., & Dunn, E. W. (2019). Valuing time over money is associated with greater social connection. *Journal of Social and Personal Relationships, 36*(8), 2549–2565. https://doi.org/10.1177/0265407518791322

22 Layous, K., Kurtz, J., Chancellor. J., & Lyubomirsky, S. (2018). Reframing the ordinary: Imagining time as scarce increases well-being. *The Journal of Positive Psychology, 13*(3), 301–308. http://doi.org/10.1080/17439760.2017.1279210

23 Whillans, A. V., Dunn, E. W., & Norton, M. I. (2018). Overcoming barriers to time-saving: Reminders of future busyness encourage consumers to buy time. *Social Influence*, 13(2), 117–124. https://doi.org/10.1080/15534510.2018.1453866

24 Kasser, T., & Sheldon, K. M. (2008). Time affluence as a path toward personal happiness and ethical business practice: Empirical evidence from four studies. *Journal of Business Ethics*, 84(2), 243–255. https://doi.org/10.1007/s10551-008-9696-1

25 Mogilner, C. (2010). The pursuit of happiness: Time, money, and social connection. *Psychological Science*, 21(9), 1348–1354. https://doi.org/10.1177/0956797610380696

26 Mogilner, C., & Aaker, J. (2009). The time vs. money effect: Shifting product attitudes and decisions through personal connection. *Journal of Consumer Research*, 36(2), 277–291. https://doi.org/10.1086/597161

27 Mogilner, C., Chance, Z., & Norton, M. I. (2012). Giving time gives you time. *Psychological Science*, 23(10), 1233–1238. https://doi.org/10.1177/0956797612442551

28 Dunn, E., & Norton, M. (2013). *Happy money: The science of happier spending* (Chapter 3, p. 61). Simon & Schuster.

29 Dunn & Norton (2013), Chapter 3, p. 62.

30 Nisbet, E. K., & Zelenski, J. M. (2011). Underestimating nearby nature: Affective forecasting errors obscure the happy path to sustainability. *Psychological Science*, 22(9), 1101–1106. https://doi.org/10.1177/0956797611418527

31 Mochon, D., Norton, M. I., & Ariely, D. (2008). Getting off the hedonic treadmill, one step at a time: The impact of regular religious practice and exercise on well-being. *Journal of Economic Psychology*, 29(5), 632–642. https://doi.org/10.1016/j.joep.2007.10.004

32 Parker-Pope, T. (2009, 14 December). The best walking partner: Man vs. dog. *The New York Times*. http://well.blogs.nytimes.com/2009/12/14/the-best-walking-partner-man-vs-dog.

33 Dunn, E., & Norton, M. (2013). *Happy money: The science of happier spending*. Simon & Schuster.

34 Weidman, A. C., & Dunn, E. W. (2016). The unsung benefits of material things: Material purchases provide more frequent momentary happiness than experiential purchases. *Social Psychological and Personality Science*, 7(4), 390–399. https://doi.org/10.1177/1948550615619976

35 Van Boven, L., & Gilovich, T. (2003). To do or to have? That is the question. *Journal of Personality and Social Psychology*, 85(6), 1193–1202. https://doi.org/10.1037/0022-3514.85.6.1193

36 Howell, R. T., & Hill, G. (2009). The mediators of experiential purchases: Determining the impact of psychological needs satisfaction and social comparison. *Journal of Positive Psychology*, 4(6), 511–522. https://doi.org/10.1080/17439760903270993

37 Carter, T. J., & Gilovich, T. (2012). I am what I do, not what I have: The differential centrality of experiential and material purchases to the self. *Journal of Personality and Social Psychology*, 102(6), 1304–1317. https://doi.org/10.1037/a0027407

38 Walker, W. R., & Skowronski, J. (2009). The fading affect bias: But what the hell is it for? *Applied Cognitive Psychology*, 23(8), 1122–1136. https://doi.org/10.1002/acp.1614

39 Mitchell, T. R., Thompson, L., Peterson, E., & Cronk, R. (1997). Temporal adjustments in the evaluation of events: The "rosy view." *Journal of Experimental Social Psychology, 33*(4), 421–448. https://doi.org/10.1006/jesp.1997.1333

40 Quoidbach, J., & Dunn, E. W. (2013). Give it up: A strategy for combating hedonic adaptation. *Social Psychological and Personality Science, 4*(5), 563–568. https://doi.org/10.1177/1948550612473489

41 Dunn, E., & Norton, M. (2013). *Happy money: The science of happier spending.* Simon & Schuster.

42 Dunn & Norton (2013).

43 Naeijn, J., Marchand, M. A., Veenhoven, R., & Vingerhoets, A. J. (2010). Vacationers happier, but most not happier after a holiday. *Applied Research in Quality of Life, 5*(1), 35–47. https://doi.org/10.1007/s11482-009-9091-9

44 Knutson, B., & Peterson, R. (2005). Neurally reconstructing expected utility. *Games and Economic Behavior, 52*(2), 305–315. https://doi.org/10.1016/j.geb.2005.01.002

45 Dunn, E., & Norton, M. (2013). *Happy money: The science of happier spending.* Simon & Schuster.

46 Dunn, E. W., Whillans, A. V., Norton, M. I., & Aknin, L. B. (2020). Prosocial spending and buying time: Money as a tool for increasing subjective well-being. In B. Gawronski (Ed.), *Advances in experimental social psychology* (Vol. 61, pp. 67–126). Elsevier.

47 Aknin, L. B., Dunn, E. W., Proulx, J., Lok, I., & Norton, M. I. (2020). Does spending money on others promote happiness? A registered replication report. *Journal of Personality and Social Psychology, 119* (2), e15–e26. http://doi.org/10.1037/pspa0000191

48 Dunn, E. W., Aknin, L. B., & Norton, M. I. (2008). Spending money on others promotes happiness. *Science, 319* (5870), 1687–1688. https://doi.org/10.1126/science.1150952

49 Dunn et al. (2008).

50 Dunn et al. (2008).

51 Aknin, L. B., Barrington-Leigh, C. P., Dunn, E. W., Helliwell, J. F., Burns, J., Biswas-Diener, R., … & Norton, M. I. (2013). Prosocial spending and well-being: Cross-cultural evidence for a psychological universal. *Journal of Personality and Social Psychology, 104*(4), 635–652. https://doi.org/10.1037/a0031578

52 Dunn, E. W., Aknin, L. B., & Norton, M. I. (2014). Prosocial spending and happiness: Using money to benefit others pays off. *Current Directions in Psychological Science, 23*(1), 41–47. https://doi.org/10.1177/0963721413512503

53 Dunn, E. W., Aknin, L. B., & Norton, M. I. (2014). Prosocial spending and happiness: Using money to benefit others pays off Corrigendum. *Current Directions in Psychological Science, 23*(2), 155. https://doi.org/10.1177/0963721414525911

54 Aknin, L. B., Fleerackers, A. L., & Hamlin, J. K. (2014). Can third-party observers detect the emotional rewards of generous spending? *The Journal of Positive Psychology, 9*(3), 198–203. https://doi.org/10.1080/17439760.2014.888578

55 Aknin, L. B. (2015). Prosocial behavior and person change. In K. J. Reynolds, N. R. Branscombe, K. J. Reynolds, & N. R. Branscombe (Eds.), *Psychology of change: Life contexts, experiences, and identities* (pp. 209–224). Psychology Press.

56 Chance, Z., & Norton, M. I. (2013). I give, therefore I have: Giving and subjective wealth, cited as a working paper at Yale University in Dunn, E. W., & Norton, M. I. (2013), *Happy money: The science of happier spending* (see chapter 5, p. 125).

57 Keyes, C. M. (2009). Toward a science of mental health. In S. J. Lopez & C. R. Snyder (Eds.), *Oxford handbook of positive psychology* (2nd ed., pp. 89–95). Oxford University Press.

58 Keyes, C. M., & Haidt, J. (Eds.). (2003). *Flourishing: Positive psychology and the life well-lived.* American Psychological Association.

59 Keyes, C. L. M., & Lopez, S. J. (2002). Toward a science of mental health: Positive directions in diagnosis and interventions. In C. R. Snyder & S. J. Lopez (Eds.), *Handbook of positive psychology* (pp. 45–59). Oxford University Press.

60 Keyes & Lopez (2002).

61 Kasser, T., & Ryan, R. M. (1993). A dark side of the American dream: Correlates of financial success as a central life aspiration. *Journal of Personality and Social Psychology, 65*(2), 410–422. https://doi.org/10.1037/0022-3514.65.2.410

62 Kasser, T., & Ryan, R. M. (1996). Further examining the American dream: Differential correlates of intrinsic and extrinsic goals. *Personality and Social Psychology Bulletin, 22*(3), 280–286. https://doi.org/10.1177/0146167296223006

63 Kasser, T. (2011). *High price of materialism.* Animated video. Center for the New American Dream. www.newdream.org.

64 Elias, M. (2002, 9 December). Ask "Dr. Happiness." *USA Today,* p. 11D.

65 Kasser, T. (2002). *The high price of materialism.* MIT Press.

66 Brickman, P. T., & Campbell, D. T. (1971). Hedonic relativism and planning the good society. In M. H. Apley (Ed.), *Adaption level theory: A symposium* (pp. 287–302). Academic Press.

67 Brickman, P., Coates, D., & Janoff-Bulman, R. (1978). Lottery winners and accident victims: Is happiness relative? *Journal of Personality and Social Psychology, 36*(8), 917–927. https://doi.org/10.1037/0022-3514.36.8.917

68 Brickman et al. (1978).

69 Wilson, T. D., & Gilbert, D. T. (2003). Affective forecasting. In M. P. Zanna (Ed.), *Advances in experimental social psychology* (pp. 345–411). Elsevier Academic Press.

70 Wilson, T. D., & Gilbert, D. T. (2005). Affective forecasting: Knowing what to want. *Current Directions in Psychological Science, 14*(3), 131–134. https://doi.org/10.1111/j.0963-7214.2005.00355.x

71 Lucas, R. E., Clark, A. E., Georgellis, Y., & Diener, E. (2004). Unemployment alters the set point for life satisfaction. *Psychological Science, 15*(1), 8–13. https://doi.org/10.1111/j.0963-7214.2004.01501002.x

72 Lucas, R. E. (2007). Adaptation and the set-point model of subjective well-being: Does happiness change after major life events? *Current Directions in Psychological Science, 16*(2), 75–79. https://doi.org/10.1111/j.1467-8721.2007.00479.x

73 Lucas, R. E. (2007). Long-term disability is associated with lasting changes in subjective well-being: Evidence from two nationally representative longitudinal studies. *Journal of Personality and Social Psychology, 92*(4), 717–730. https://doi.org/10.1037/0022-3514.92.4.717

74 Kasser, T. (2002). *The high price of materialism.* MIT Press.

75 Fredrickson, B. L. (1998). What good are positive emotions? *Review of General Psychology, 2,* 300–319. doi:10.1037/1089-2680.2.3.300

76 Froh, J. J. (2009). Positive emotions. In S. J. Lopez (Ed.), *The encyclopedia of positive psychology* (Vol. II, pp. 711–717). Wiley-Blackwell.

77 Conway, A. M., Tugade, M. M., Catalino, L. I., & Fredrickson, B. L. (2013). The broaden-and-build theory of positive emotions: Form, function, and mechanisms. In S. A. David, I. Boniwell, & A. Conley Ayers (Eds.), *The Oxford handbook of happiness* (pp. 17–34). Oxford University Press.

78 Fredrickson, B. L. (1998). What good are positive emotions? *Review of General Psychology, 2*, 300–319. doi:10.1037/1089-2680.2.3.300.

79 Fredrickson, B. L. (2002). Positive emotions. In C. R. Snyder & S. J. Lopez (Eds.), *Handbook of positive psychology* (pp. 120–134). Oxford University Press.

80 Fredrickson, B. L., & Branigan, C. (2005). Positive emotions broaden the scope of attention of thought and behavior. *Cognition and Emotion, 19*(3), 313–332. https://doi.org/10.1080/02699930441000238

81 Fredrickson, B. L. (2002). Positive emotions. In C. R. Snyder & S. J. Lopez (Eds.), *Handbook of positive psychology* (pp. 120–134). Oxford University Press.

82 Fredrickson, B. L., & Joiner, T. (2005). Positive emotions trigger upward spirals toward emotional well-being. *Psychological Science, 13*(2), 172–175. https://doi.org/10.1111/1467-9280.00431

83 Watkins, P. C. (2014). *Gratitude and the good life: Toward a psychology of appreciation*. Springer.

84 Armenta, C. N., Fritz, M. M., & Lyubomirsky, S. (2016). Functions of positive emotions: Gratitude as a motivator of self-improvement and positive change. *Emotion Review*, 1–8. https://doi.org/10.1177/1754073916669596

85 Larsen, R. J., & Prizmic, Z. (2008). Regulation of emotional well-being: Overcoming the hedonic treadmill. In M. Eid & R. J. Larsen (Eds.), *The science of subjective well-being* (pp. 258–289). Guilford.

86 Algoe, S. B., & Haidt, J. (2009). Witnessing excellence in action: The "other-praising" emotions of elevation, gratitude, and admiration. *Journal of Positive Psychology, 4* (2), 105–127. https://doi.org/10.1080/17439760802650519

87 Ko, K., Margolis, S., Revord, J., & Lyubomirsky, S. (2019). Comparing the effects of performing and recalling acts of kindness. *The Journal of Positive Psychology.* https://doi.org/10.1080/17439760.2019.1663252

88 Emmons, R. A., & McCullough, M. E. (2003). Counting blessings versus burdens: Experimental studies of gratitude and subjective well-being in daily life. *Journal of Personality and Social Psychology, 84*, 377–389. https://doi.org/10.1037/0022-3514.84.2.377

89 Seligman, M. E. P., Steen, T. A., Park, N., & Peterson, C. (2005). Positive psychology progress: Empirical validation of interventions. *American Psychologist, 60*, 410–421.

90 Peterson, C. (2006). *A primer in positive psychology* (p. 38). Oxford University Press.

91 Maisel, N., & Gable, S. (2009). For richer ... in good times ... and in health: Positive processes in relationships. In C. R. Snyder & S. J. Lopez (Eds.), *Oxford handbook of positive psychology* (2nd ed., pp. 455–462). Oxford University Press.

92 Gable, S. L., Reis, H. T., Impett, E. A., & Asher, E. R. (2004). What do you do when things go right? The intrapersonal and interpersonal benefits of sharing positive events. *Journal of Personality and Social Psychology, 87*(2), 228–245. https://doi.org/10.1037/0022-3514.87.2.228

93 Bryant, F. B., & Veroff, J. (2007). *Savoring: A new model of positive experience.* Erlbaum.

94 Vohs, K. D., Mead, N. L., & Goode, M. R. (2006). The psychological consequences of money. *Science, 314*(5802), 1154–1156. https://doi.org/10.1126/science.1132491.

95 Brown, K. W., & Ryan, R. M. (2003). The benefits of being present: Mindfulness and its role in psychological well-being. *Journal of Personality and Social Psychology, 84*(4), 822–848. https://doi.org/10.1037/0022-3514.84.4.822

96 Jose, P. E., Lim, B. T., & Bryant, F. B. (2012). Does savoring increase happiness? A daily diary study. *The Journal of Positive Psychology, 7*(3), 176–187. https://doi.org/10.1080/17439760.2012.671345

97 Hurley, D. B., & Kwan, P. (2012). Results of a study to increase savoring the moment: Differential impact on positive and negative outcomes. *Journal of Happiness Studies, 13*(4), 579–588. https://doi.org/10.1007/s10902-011-9280-8

98 Heintzelman, S. J., & King, L. A. (2014). Life is pretty meaningful. *American Psychologist, 69,* 561–574. https://doi.org/10.1037/a0035049

99 Heintzelman & King (2014).

100 Hicks, J. A., & King, L. A. (2009). Meaning in life as a judgment and lived experience. *Social and Personality Psychology Compass, 3*(4), 638–653. doi:10.1111/j.1751-9004.2009.00193.x

101 Steger, M. F., & Kashdan, T. B. (2009). Depression and everyday social activity, intimacy, and well-being. *Journal of Counseling Psychology, 56*(2), 289–300. https://doi.org/10.1037/a0015416

102 Krause, N. (2007). Longitudinal study of social support and meaning in life. *Psychology and Aging, 22*(3), 456–469. https://doi:10.1037/0882-7974.22.3.456

103 Steger, M. F., Mann, J. R., Michels, P., & Cooper, T. C. (2009). Meaning in life, anxiety, depression, and general health among smoking cessation patients. *Journal of Psychosomatic Research, 67*(4), 353–358. https://doi.org/10.1016/j.jpsychores.2009.02.006

104 Boyle, P. A., Buchman, A. S., Barnes, L. L., & Bennett, D. A. (2010). Effect of a purpose in life on risk of incident Alzheimer disease and mild cognitive impairment in community-dwelling older persons. *Archives of General Psychiatry, 67*(3), 304–310. https://doi.org/10.1001/archgenpsychiatry.2009.208

105 Williams, K. S. (2007). Ostracism. *Annual Review of Psychology, 58,* 425–452.

106 Boyle, P. A., Barnes, L. L., Buchman, A. S., & Bennett, D. A. (2009). Purpose in life is associated with mortality among community-dwelling older persons. *Psychosomatic Medicine, 71*(5), 574–579. https://doi.org/10.1097/PSY.0b013e3181a5a7c0

107 Littman-Ovadia, H., & Steger, M. (2010). Character strengths and well-being among volunteers and employees. *Journal of Positive Psychology, 5*(6), 419–430. https://doi.org/10.1080/17439760.2010.516765

108 Stillman, T. F., Lambert, N. M., Fincham, F. D., & Baumeister, R. F. (2011). Meaning as a magnetic force: Evidence that meaning in life promotes interpersonal appeal. *Social Psychological and Personality Science, 2*(1), 13–20. https://doi.org/10.1177/1948550610378382

109 Thompson, N. J., Coker, J., Krause, J. S., & Henry, E. (2003). Pure in life as a mediator of adjustment after spinal cord injury. *Rehabilitation Psychology, 48*(2), 100–108. https://doi.org/10.1037/0090-5550.48.2.100

110 Heintzelman, S. J., & King, L. A. (2014). Life is pretty meaningful. *American Psychologist, 69,* 561–574. https://doi.org/10.1037/a0035049.

111 Heintzelman & King (2014), p. 569.

112 Diener, E., Wirtz, D., Tov, W., Kim-Prieto, C., Choi, D., Oishi, S., & Biswas-Diener, R. (2010). New well-being measures: Short scales to assess flourishing and positive and negative feelings. *Social Indicators Research, 97*(2), 143–156. https://doi.org/10.1007/s11205-009-9493-y

113 Bryant, F. B., & Veroff, J. (2007). *Savoring: A new model of positive experience.* Erlbaum.

114 Bryant, F. (1989). A four-factor model of perceived control: Avoiding, coping, obtaining, and savoring. *Journal of Personality, 57*(4), 773–797. https://doi.org/ :10.1111/j.1467-6494.1989.tb00494.x

115 Steger, M. F., Frazier, P., Oishi, S., & Kaler, M. (2006). The Meaning in Life Questionnaire: Assessing the presence of and search for meaning in life. *Journal of Counseling Psychology, 53*, 80–93. https://doi.org/10.1037/022-0167.53.1.80

Section 4   My relationships

How do relationships affect our lives? Some people might argue that relationships affect every aspect of our lives. Some may even believe that we must engage with other people so that we can meet our daily needs. We might interact directly with another person or electronically through the multitude of formats available today. We may choose to interact with another person to meet a more basic emotional need. In either case, relationships are central to the health, happiness, and enjoyment of our lives.

Part 4.1 Relationships – it takes all kinds

We have many different types of relationships. In some instances, our interactions are merely pragmatic or transactional. For example, we frequently interact with people for a specific purpose – such as buying the newest cellphone, clothing, or groceries. Of course, we are increasingly interacting electronically instead of directly with another person as more communication is being conducted online. Nevertheless, even in these simple exchanges conducted for mundane purposes, communicating is both essential and complex. We must find ways to obtain a desired outcome, yet the words that we use, the body language that we express, our tone of voice, and volume of our expression influence communication. Regardless of how we communicate, a successful outcome is critical if we are to survive because if there is a miscommunication, it is possible that we fail to obtain one of the basic necessities of life (e.g., food, shelter). Thus, at this very pragmatic level, communication is essential to survival.

Transactional interactions allow us to engage in the daily activities of everyday life. In other words, **evolutionary psychologists** suggest that today, survival requires some form of communication to meet the basic needs for food and shelter. Although these types of interactions are seemingly straightforward, a number of individual factors influence our relationships. For example, we typically interact differently with people based on their gender, age, or a host of demographic variables. Why did these patterns of communication emerge? Very early in agrarian cultures social interaction stratified relationships on the basis of gender. Women worked together to care for children and to perform less physically demanding work (e.g., preparing food), and men developed relationships and they performed more physically demanding

DOI: 10.4324/9781003188711-5

tasks. Today however, most work is not physically demanding and this type of gender stratification is no longer necessary. Yet, gender stereotypes continue to be reinforced in cultures across the world, and these interactions continue to shape our experiences.

As society evolved, the nature and complexity of human relationships also changed. People began to form many relationships to meet a more complex set of needs. These early pragmatic relationships may have developed for the purpose of ensuring survival, but something else was happening too. People began to derive satisfaction, or an intrinsic benefit from their interactions with others. In other words, people found meaning in sharing experiences. They also worked together for the purpose of ensuring basic survival, and they were deriving benefits that helped them to feel better.

Although we may have intuitively recognized the importance of relationships, it wasn't until the 20th century, when the discipline of psychology was born, that we were able to begin to study the role of relationships in overall health. **Psychology** is the study of the neurological, physical, emotional, intellectual, cognitive functioning of human beings. Thus, it is this complex set of factors that explains the importance of relationships for our survival, health, and well-being. In other words, psychological health is one element of our overall physical health. So, positive and negative experiences influence our psychological well-being, and the positive relationships allow us to live healthier and emotionally more satisfying lives. In this section we consider the complex set of factors that affect our lives and the role of relationships in the psychological health.

Part 4.2 Emotions and relationships are closely intertwined

As we illustrated earlier, transactional interactions are essential for conducting our daily activities, but a more important, deeper connection to other people is fundamental to human health. Let's think about the many types of experiences we have on a daily basis. Every day we encounter dozens of people and even a casual interaction with someone we barely know, may have important consequences. For example, if someone says, "you look nice today," it is likely to result in a positive feeling. Although psychologists are not entirely clear about how we process emotion, this very brief encounter, and resulting positive feeling, is the result of a complex set of internal responses.

Processing emotion involves cognition, biology, and a response or feeling associated with the experience. So, the personal compliment that you received is likely processed by the prefrontal cortex or the portion of the brain that is associated with thinking, and the *limbic system* or the portion of the brain associated with emotion. We process experiences very quickly, so the speed at which neural activation occurs makes it difficult to determine exactly which process happens first, cognition or emotion. But it is likely that a personal compliment, or positive emotion, is processed first by the brain's prefrontal cortex, or cognitive processing center. From there, the brain sends a message to the **amygdala** (emotion control center) and **neurotransmitters** (i.e., endorphins) are released. In other words, even this brief and seemingly insignificant interaction results in a positive emotional and physical experience. Hundreds of interactions occur daily and each results in an outcome that can have compounding positive or negative effects on our overall health and well-being.

If a single compliment generates this complex reaction and positive feeling, what happens when we have a negative interaction with another person? Depending on the type or intensity of the experience, an unpleasant interaction may result in significant negative consequences that are likely to affect our long-term physical and emotional health. For example, if instead of receiving a compliment, someone tells you that you are unlikely to succeed in a class, a slightly different set of reactions occur. In all likelihood, this type of information elicits an uncomfortable response that might be characterized as anger, anxiety, or sadness. If you feel threatened, then fear might be the emotion that you experience. Fear is processed more quickly because it triggers a neurological shortcut to allow the body to respond quickly.[1] Rather than processing this information in the prefrontal cortex first, a stimulus that elicits fear activates the **amygdala** (emotion control center) almost immediately, resulting in the release of different hormones (i.e., adrenalin, noradrenalin) that help the person deal with a threat. As you might imagine, ongoing negative experiences take their toll on us. In fact, long-term exposure to stressful events results in decreased immune system function.

The human body is designed to benefit from positive human interactions, and we possess physiological and psychological coping mechanisms that help us to deal with negative experiences. So, more frequent positive experiences result in better long-term health.

Earlier we referenced the value of working together in an agrarian society to meet the most basic of human needs – eating. We also noted that more sophisticated social structures continued to develop throughout the centuries. Almost every culture has social structures that allow people to meet and share experiences. Schools, churches, and clubs are just a few of the many socially constructed groups that provide us with opportunities to meet our psychological needs for affiliation.

Early in our lives we interact with friends in school, and social groups that are typically associated with school-age children. These early experiences shape our ability to form relationships and interact effectively with people around us. Uri Bronfenbrenner emphasized the importance of the environment on human development in his **bioecological systems theory**.[2] He suggested that children are directly influenced most strongly by immediate family, and that the social systems surrounding the family are also important (e.g., school, peer groups, social networks). Together with Ceci they emphasized the importance of both social institutions and biological forces in the development of healthy people.[3] Regardless of culture or age, social relationships are an important predictor of happiness,[4] so it is important to have strong positive social networks.

Throughout our lives the types of groups we affiliate with change based on our interests and needs. As young children we may have joined the scouts, played soccer, or participated as a member of the chess club. As young adults, there are opportunities to join fraternities, sororities, or college sports. In some cases, groups may be exclusive, so not everyone can belong or participate. Yet, the need to belong is fundamental to our survival.[5] Everyone experiences rejection at some point in their life, and this emotion not only feels bad, but as we noted earlier, it can have negative consequences on our health.

Think about the time you may have been excluded from a group because you weren't perceived as capable of playing a sport, or perhaps you could not join a club because you weren't liked by the current members. Dewall and Bushman[6] explored the role of social rejection and they found that exclusion affects virtually every aspect of our being – cognitive, behavioral, and neural. They also found that social rejection profoundly affects our ability to lead a healthy and productive life because as rejection increases, anxiety, depression, anger, and sadness are likely to increase.

Why is rejection so powerful? Researchers have long been interested in understanding the connection between biology and emotion. With recent developments in brain imagining, scientists are now able to investigate this relationship with increasing accuracy. We already know that there is a connection between an experience, the limbic system, and the release of hormones. Additional clarification for the linkage between emotion and the physiological response may partially be explained by the perception of physical pain. Evolutionary factors may be at work here. If social interaction is crucial for survival, then social rejection results in a negative physiological reaction. In fact, many researchers[7,8] found just that; rejection results in both emotional and physical pain. Our body tries to counteract the pain by releasing endorphins, or neurotransmitters that serve to reduce the level of pain we are feeling. Endorphins are the body's naturally occurring opiates that work by blocking the communication of painful experiences to the brain. So, regardless of whether the pain is physical or emotional, the neurological reaction, or release of endorphins, helps to counteract the feelings of pain.[9]

Pain is often treated with medications. For example, if you get a headache, you are likely to take some type of over-the-counter medication. DeWall and Bushman conducted a study to test whether this same type of medication might reduce emotional pain. In fact, they found that something as simple as acetaminophen can reduce painful feelings associated with rejection. Individuals cope with rejection a number of ways including seeking out new relationships.

If social rejection or isolation is unhealthy, can we conclude that increasing social relationships results in better health? Researchers found support for this assertion. Diener and Seligman[10] found that people with strong social relationships are happier. They also reported that if people have a basic level of financial security, then social relationships are related to happiness even more than money.[11]

What is the optimal level of social interaction? There is no single formula that predicts exactly how much social interaction is beneficial for human health. The perception of social inclusion and relationships is highly personal. Nevertheless, our species has evolved such that some level of positive human interaction is essential for survival. These concepts continuously overlap between health and happiness, as any careful reader of this book will discover. In fact, some researchers[12] have developed a model to attempt to capture/measure these interrelationships; the AIM approach (pp. 202–203). The AIM approach to happiness involves three main concepts: A = attention, I = interpretation, and M = memory. Individuals who are uncharacteristically happy often seek the position (<u>a</u>ttending), observe neutral outcomes as positive and find growth opportunities when adversity occurs (<u>i</u>nterpreting), and they tend to reminisce about a positive past (<u>r</u>emembering). To see how the AIM approach works, complete the exercise presented in Table 4.1.

From the researchers: If you find yourself agreeing with many of the negative thinking statements and disagreeing with many of the positive thinking statements, it is time to change. Remember, thinking is like any other habit – it can be changed with effort. And remember that if you are a negative thinker, this is not because this is the way the world truly is, but is in the way you

Table 4.1 Measuring your AIM

Check each statement that applies to you, then add the number of checks in each section.

Negative thinking

_____ I quickly notice the mistakes made by others.
_____ I often see the faults in other people.
_____ I see my community as a place full of problems.
_____ When I think of myself, I think of many shortcomings.
_____ When somebody does something for me, I usually wonder if they have an ulterior motive.
_____ When good things happen, I wonder if they will soon turn sour.
_____ When good things happen, I wonder if they might have been better.
_____ When I see others prosper, it makes me feel bad about myself.
_____ I frequently compare myself to others.
_____ I think frequently about the opportunities that I missed.
_____ I regret many things from my past.
_____ When I think of the past, for some reason bad things stand out.
_____ When something bad happens, I ruminate on it for a long time.
_____ Most people will take advantage of you if you give them the slightest chance.

Positive thinking

_____ I see much beauty around me.
_____ I see the good in most people.
_____ I believe in the good qualities of other people.
_____ I think of myself as a person with many strengths.
_____ When something bad happens, I often see a "silver lining," something good in the bad event.
_____ I sometimes think about how fortunate I have been in life.
_____ When I think of the past, the happy times are most salient to me.
_____ I savor memories of pleasant past times.
_____ When I see others prosper, even strangers, I am happy for them.
_____ I notice the little good things others do.
_____ I know the world has problems, but it seems like a wonderful place anyway.
_____ I see many opportunities in the world.
_____ I am optimistic about the future.

Interpretation

Here are some guidelines for interpreting your answers:

Negative thinking	Low 1–4	Medium 5–9	High 10–14
Positive thinking	Low 1–4	Medium 5–8	High 9–13

---

choose to see that world. If you scored high on positive thinking and low on negative thinking, you are in the long run very likely to be basically a happy person. If your negative score is higher than your positive score, you have developed a negative way of thinking about yourself, the world, and others. You should evaluate whether this approach actually works for you, or whether you might function more effectively with more positivity.

Part 4.3 Does "one" have to be a lonely number?

When we do not have the opportunity to interact socially we might feel lonely. Loneliness is an individual perception of a feeling of "disconnectedness" from a social support system. In other words, the feeling of loneliness is essentially the discrepancy between desired and actual social interactions.[13] Yet, loneliness is not the same as being alone. Many people enjoy being alone, and as long as they have some form of social interaction, they report high levels of happiness.

As we noted earlier, loneliness is associated with reported feelings of pain and increased physical and mental health problems.[14,15] Lonely people have a higher incidence of cardiovascular problems and increased mortality. Cognitive performance also declines with perceived feelings of loneliness. Hawkley and Cacioppo have a loneliness model in which they suggest that when people feel lonely they become hypervigilant, they attend to negative social interactions with more frequency, and their negative expectations result in a **self-fulfilling prophecy** that only increases the feelings of loneliness. If we subscribe to a self-fulfilling prophecy, or a belief about ourselves, then we will act in a way that is consistent with our belief. Our actions may in turn result in outcomes that we expect and reinforce our original (negative) perception of ourselves. In other words, the self-fulfilling prophecy results in a vicious cycle that only serves to increase our feelings of loneliness.

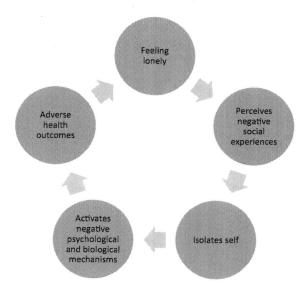

Because loneliness can have devastating effects on overall health, it is important to find ways to help people feel more connected. In a comprehensive review of the literature Cacioppo and his colleagues[16] found that individual treatment interventions, counseling or psychotherapy, are only moderately effective at reducing loneliness. Aaron Beck is the founder of cognitive therapy and it is used to treat a number of disorders very effectively. Individual CBT, or cognitive therapy – changing an individual's perception, has only limited success because it is difficult for people to change their automatic negative thoughts.

So, how do we help people break the cycle that perpetuates the loneliness? Getting people engaged in a social support program offers some promise. The most successful social support programs involve a shared sense of responsibility (e.g., engaging in a mentoring program). In other words, if someone is feeling lonely, then it is important to get the person involved in some type of experience that requires the person to engage with others. For example, volunteering involves responsibility and will likely help reduce feelings of loneliness.

Will being alone result in negative outcomes or feelings of loneliness? People routinely make choices about how much time to spend in social situations. These choices are influenced by many factors including an individual's personality, social status, or available opportunities. Eysenck originally proposed a trait theory of personality that included just two factors – an introverted/extraverted dimension and an unstable/stable dimension. This theory was later expanded to reflect what we now consider the **five-factor trait theory/Big Five theory of personality** (i.e., conscientiousness, agreeableness, neuroticism, openness, and extraversion).[17] Although a single theory cannot account for every aspect of personality, this theory suggests that we can classify people on five basic dimensions that are relatively stable.[18] The five traits are conscientiousness, agreeableness, openness, neuroticism, and extraversion. The conscientiousness trait reflects a tendency to achieve, persist, and engage in self-control. Agreeableness reflects cooperative behaviors. Openness is the dimension that reflects a range of flexibility. Neuroticism reflects the level of anxiety. Finally, extraversion reflects the dimension or level of sociability that one may feel.

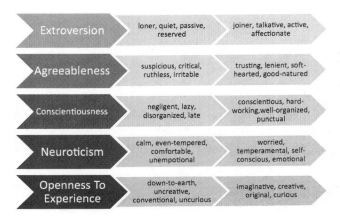

Big Five[19]

Although there is not yet consensus on the definitive number of personality traits,[20] there is general agreement that Eysenck's basic traits generally reflect personality dimensions. For example, some people may tend to be either introverts or extroverts. In other words, people may prefer to be less sociable (introverted) than social (extraverted). So, our willingness to engage in social activities is related to where we fall on the extraversion dimension. If we are more introverted, then we may prefer to spend more time alone, while at the same time, being alone doesn't feel lonely.

Being a loner is completely different from choosing to be alone, or feeling lonely. A loner deliberately chooses not to form close relationships. This type of existence may have developed early in an individual's life as a result of poor attachment with a care giver. Negative social interactions (e.g., bullying) may have resulted in psychological pain. Psychologists do not fully understand why individuals become social isolated, but we do know that people without a connection to society are more likely to engage in behaviors that are anti-social. In fact, Dewall and Bushman[21] examined the profiles of people who were mass shooters and found that almost all of the individuals had experienced some form of social rejection. When individuals experience social rejection, they have the typical set of negative feelings and physiological responses. The difference is that for some individuals, those that are particularly sensitive to social rejection, these feelings result in aggression. Thus, an individual may feel ostracized, become a loner, and in rare instances, they may act on their feelings of aggression.

When we consider the distinctions between feelings of loneliness, being alone, and becoming a loner, it is important to note that there is one additional group of individuals who may simply be incapable of forming social connections. For reasons we don't fully understand, **autism spectrum disorder** (ASD) is a condition that significantly limits an individual from understanding social relationships and limits meaningful social interactions. Researchers have recently shared that the etiology of the disorder is neurodevelopmental in nature and likely involves some element of genetic predisposition.[22,23] So, the ability to form relationships for someone with ASD is significantly constrained.

Part 4.4 All in the family (attachment)

Thus far we have learned that staying connected helps us to live a richer and happier life. So, we might ask, how do we develop and maintain positive relationships? This really is not a simple question as there are many different factors that affect the quality of relationships. For example, early experiences shape who we become and how we interact with the world. From the moment we are born, we have a need to connect with another human being. Psychologists labeled this need "attachment," or the first bonding of a child with a caregiver, as essential for survival.

One of the earliest and most important studies of attachment was conducted by Harry and Margaret Harlow.[24] Because monkeys are similar to humans, they created an experiment to study how monkeys developed early in life. Both Harlow researchers separated infant monkeys from their mothers almost immediately after they were born. Through highly controlled experimental conditions, they found that the infant monkeys needed soft nurturing contact, in addition to food, for their survival.

Building on this work, researchers found that this same need for nurturing is also present in human infants. Ainsworth extended Harlow's research and conducted the seminal study of human attachment in infants. She found that infants who had a secure attachment to their mother were able to form better relationships. Similarly, for those children who had not formed a positive attachment (insecure attachment) with their mother, they had higher levels of anxiety and difficulty forming relationships.[25,26]

Unfortunately, researchers conducting naturalistic studies provide even more evidence that attachment is crucial for developing an ability to form healthy relationships. In several countries children are abandoned and grow up in orphanages. Children growing up in these conditions experience many difficulties including a reduced ability to form strong positive relationships. So, early childhood experiences may result in lifelong outcomes that affect the ability to form relationships. Researchers studied the long-lasting effects associated with an inability to form a secure attachment in early childhood.[27] Although the research into this area is ongoing, preliminary results suggest that there may be a relationship between early attachment style and our relationships later in life.

Our needs and capacity for developing relationships continues to evolve as we enter the earliest stages of childhood. Children are developing an ability to think in increasingly complex ways, while at the same time, they are continuing to experience a wider set of social relationships. For example, young children begin to expand their social networks as they have opportunities to play with their peers. As toddlers, they are beginning to discover that they can do things independently. These experiences and insights allow a child to develop a sense of autonomy. Erik Erikson conducted the seminal research on how children develop socially. He suggested that we move through an age-related sequence of tasks, which allows us to develop increasingly sophisticated levels of social interaction.[28]

At the same time young children are continuing to develop intellectually and beginning to develop an understanding of perspectives that might be unique to someone else. The cognitive development that is occurring at the same time is what Premack and Woodruff labeled the **theory of mind**.[29] It is this understanding of the perspectives of another person that is so important for healthy relationships throughout life. Children also begin to understand the principle of social reciprocity – if someone helps us, we should help them. It is important to understand social reciprocity if a child is to develop healthy relationships throughout life.[30]

As you might imagine, we continue to develop increasingly sophisticated ways of thinking and interacting as we get older. At adolescence we are exploring our sense of identity – who we are becoming. Together with the internal factors that are helping us to develop this sense of self, we are affiliating with social groups and finding our place within society. Until we reach early adulthood, our self-concept and our social affiliations are somewhat fluid, but as we reach adulthood, we have a much clearer sense of ourselves and we are able to form long-lasting relationships.

We form many types of relationships – friends, family, work, social groups, and romantic partners. Regardless of the type of relationship, there are many things that influence our relationships. Perhaps one of the most important factors is **proximity**. If we have an opportunity to interact with someone frequently, we tend to like them more. In fact, we now recognize the **mere exposure effect** as a phenomenon that suggests that we tend to like an individual more if we interact more frequently. For example, today we are much more mobile than we were a century ago. You may have noticed that a once close friendship may decline over time if you move to another town. So, our physical proximity and frequency of interaction is related to the strength of our feelings toward the person. Proximity is particularly important in developing a relationship with a romantic partner.

Part 4.5 O partner my partner

Erikson suggested that we have a need for intimacy which leads to the search for a romantic partner early in adulthood. As people mature into adults they generally have a clearer sense of identity which allows them to develop a significant relationship. The relationship, or partnering, may develop out of a physical attraction, but it is sustained through caring and a shared sense of relationship. For the most part, a romantic partner allows us to lead a healthier life. Partners can share financial resources, but more importantly, they can share feelings and support each other during difficult times. This long-term relationship offers great benefits for keeping us healthy and increasing our satisfaction with life.

There are many factors at play when we are searching for a romantic partner. As noted earlier, proximity is important in developing the relationship. **Similarity**, or a common set of experiences and values, will allow a relationship to grow stronger. For example, if we connect with a person who understands our experience growing up in a small town, then we share a common sense of identity and understanding. A shared understanding on important dimensions (e.g., education, religion, intelligence, and economic status) serves to strengthen a relationship.

Let's take a closer look at the role of physical attractiveness as a factor in developing relationships. Although we may not want to believe that we are influenced by physical attractiveness, the research clearly indicates that people prefer to affiliate with attractive people (i.e., the halo effect[31]). Features that define physical attractiveness are not always culturally bound. Researchers believe that facial symmetry, average physical features (not too large, not too small), and healthy-looking people are preferred regardless of race.[32] Proximity, similarity, and physical attractiveness are just three of the factors that are influential in our decisions about who we chose as a romantic partner.

Although we tend to develop a relationship with a significant other in early adulthood, there are many reasons why partnering may occur throughout life. For example, many people still believe that being gay is wrong. Yet, the evidence is clear; sexual orientation is merely a biological variation that is perfectly normal.[33] Nevertheless, people who are gay have a unique set of difficulties in searching for a romantic partner. First, they must develop a positive sense of identity and acceptance. Then, they must find ways to meet a romantic partner within a subculture that is limited in terms of access. Finally, they must learn to develop a healthy relationship despite the disapproval of many in society.

Regardless of when a romantic relationship(s) develops, the feelings of love usually progress through three stages. Passionate love is that first euphoric feeling that seems to dominate our thoughts during the early stages of a relationship. The excitement we feel during this first stage is influenced by the release of the positive hormones that we discussed earlier. Researchers indicate that the early stages of passionate love result in a host of positive outcomes including decreased levels of physical pain.[34] Just the mere sight of the partner can spark excitement and the release of hormones (e.g., testosterone, dopamine, and adrenaline) which only serves to increase feelings of well-being and a growing fondness for the partner.

Sadly, this level of passion cannot be sustained forever. After all, at some point the constant release of hormones will result in exhaustion. So, the relationship moves into a second stage – companionate love. This stage is more sustainable as the couple finds ways to support each other and share in a long-term relationship that will result in a healthier life.

The positive effects of partnering have long-term positive consequences. Researchers report that people who are in a partnered relationship live longer. The caveat is that the relationship should be generally positive.[35] Jaremka and colleagues found that a stressful marital relationship actually compromises immune function.[36] If the relationship is positive a couple can share in the pragmatic elements of life (e.g., sharing resources), and they can support each other through ongoing sharing of feelings and companionate love. However, if a relationship becomes difficult for an extended period of time, it may be better to end the relationship for the health of both partners.

Part 4.6 It's best to be positive

For most of us, social relationships are a central part of a healthy and meaningful life. When we engage in social activities, we feel better and we enjoy life more. So, in this section we present ways to maintain positive relationships, and ultimately our health. You'll actually read more about this topic in Section 3 about becoming enriched/psychological wealth and in Section 5 that focuses on happiness.

Perhaps the most important element of any relationship is **trust**. In order to build a relationship, we must feel as though we can trust another person with our feelings. If this foundational element is not present, then we will not be able develop a meaningful relationship.

A key component of maintaining positive relationships is treating others with respect. As trust develops, we feel increasing levels of intimacy. When we know someone intimately, we tend to become more comfortable around the other person and sometimes we are less attentive to our own actions. So, a deep level of understanding can result in positive or negative actions. For example, if we know that a friend or partner tends to procrastinate, then we may tend to blame the person for failing to complete a task because of their disposition. **Attributions**, that is, assigning responsibility for another's actions, can be internal or external. If we make an internal attribution about a person's behavior, then we are assuming that the person engaged in the behavior because of who they are. If we make an external attribution, then we consider the environment as a possible cause of the behavior. So, if we believe that a person failed to complete a task because he or she is just lazy, then we are making a negative internal attribution. However, there are times a person may not complete a task because of external circumstances. If we attribute the failure to the internal disposition of the individual, rather than a legitimate set of circumstances (external conditions), we are engaging in the **fundamental attribution error**. Persisting in this pattern of thinking may create tension in a relationship. In other words, we need to be caring and one way to do this is to remain attuned to our thoughts and actions.[37]

So, how can we exercise care and avoid these errors in thinking? There are no easy answers. Relationships are complex. In addition to having a relationship with a partner, as adults, we engage in many relationships that have differing levels of intimacy. For example, we typically have close friends, acquaintances, professional friendships, and relationships with members of our family, among others. Regardless of the type of relationship, we have to remain attuned to engaging in behaviors that help us maintain positive relationships. Note: In the introduction to this book there is a brief listing of logical fallacies, which is another way of saying "errors in thinking."

A third action we can take in maintaining a positive relationship is to remain aware of the need for **equity**. Relationships are reciprocal.[38] So, both members of a relationship have to be committed to devoting time and energy to the relationship. If one person is consistently initiating contact, the relationship will not survive because there is not a balance in the responsibility for maintaining the relationship.

Similarly, there must be a balance in the level of **self-disclosure**. Each of our relationships is different, so there is a range of intimacy. If the relationship is extremely intimate, then both individuals will need to share highly personal information. We also maintain fewer intimate relationships and they involve fewer disclosures. So, the level of sharing is comparable because the level of information is not as personal. Listening to emotional self-disclosures increases feelings of connectedness.[39] Ultimately, we can build more intimate relationships if we engage in reciprocal self-disclosure with a high level of trust.[40]

A healthy relationship also requires careful attention to listening and monitoring our own interactions. Carl Rogers, a humanist psychologist, suggested that we must engage in **unconditional positive regard** to maintain positive relationships. In other words, it is important to express an ongoing acceptance of an individual even though the other person may be feeling sad or unhappy.[41]

Regardless of how good a relationship might be, interpersonal conflict is almost inevitable. A conflict may simply be a misunderstanding based on poor communication. For example, someone may simply have forgotten that their partner had to work late and that they would be late getting home. In this case, unclear communication is at the source of the misunderstanding, so another important element of maintaining a good relationship is clear communication.

When a misunderstanding occurs, then it is important to navigate the problem effectively. How do we negotiate conflict within a relationship? In an interesting study designed to examine wisdom, Grossman and Koss[42] found that stepping back (reducing egocentrism) and gaining perspective helps us to see things more clearly and contributes to developing more positive relationships. So, when we find ourselves engaged in a particularly emotional interaction that might be the result of a misunderstanding, it is best to try to extract ourselves from the heat of the moment and gain perspective. This strategy reflects the old adage that things will always look better in the morning after a good night's sleep.

Our perception of an issue is likely to shape our actions. One element of perception is **locus of control**. If we are oriented with an internal locus of control, then we are empowered to take action to change the situation. If we have an external locus of control, our perception is that actions are largely defined by conditions around us. If we experience conflict, then it is important to balance our perceptions about the current set of circumstances. It is entirely likely that another person is angry and we cannot control another person's actions or feelings. But, we can control our reactions. Rather than responding directly to the other person's anger, a healthy alternative is to refocus and take positive actions that you can control. To learn more about these ideas, we present the classic locus of control scale in Table 4.2.[43]

One of the emotions that often occurs with conflict is anger. Anger activates the sympathetic nervous system, and chronic anger ultimately results in reduced cardiovascular health. Anger is a natural emotion experienced by everyone, but if left unchecked, it can have negative consequences. Thus, it is important to find ways to manage anger effectively, particularly in relationships. When we feel angry, it is best to step back from the situation and gain perspective. After taking some time to get a better understanding, it is possible to more constructively respond to the situation. Sometimes, however, it is best to end the relationship for the sake of everyone involved.

Table 4.2 Locus of control scale

For each item pair, select the statement that you agree with most.

1.
a. Children get into trouble because their parents punish them too much.
b. The trouble with most children nowadays is that their parents are too easy with them.

2.
a. Many of the unhappy things in people's lives are partly due to bad luck.
b. People's misfortunes result from the mistakes they make.

3.
a. One of the major reasons why we have wars is because people don't take enough interest in politics.
b. There will always be wars, no matter how hard people try to prevent them.

4.
a. In the long run people get the respect they deserve in this world
b. Unfortunately, an individual's worth often passes unrecognized no matter how hard he tries

5.
a. The idea that teachers are unfair to students is nonsense.
b. Most students don't realize the extent to which their grades are influenced by accidental happenings.

6.
a. Without the right breaks one cannot be an effective leader.
b. Capable people who fail to become leaders have not taken advantage of their opportunities.

7.
a. No matter how hard you try some people just don't like you.
b. People who can't get others to like them don't understand how to get along with others.

8.
a. Heredity plays the major role in determining one's personality
b. It is one's experiences in life which determine what they're like.

9.
a. I have often found that what is going to happen will happen.
b. Trusting to fate has never turned out as well for me as making a decision to take a definite course of action.

10.
a. In the case of the well-prepared student there is rarely if ever such a thing as an unfair test.
b. Many times exam questions tend to be so unrelated to course work that studying is really useless.

11.
a. Becoming a success is a matter of hard work; luck has little or nothing to do with it.
b. Getting a good job depends mainly on being in the right place at the right time.

12.
a. The average citizen can have an influence in government decisions.
b. This world is run by the few people in power, and there is not much the little guy can do about it.

Table 4.2 Cont.

13.
a. When I make plans, I am almost certain that I can make them work.
b. It is not always wise to plan too far ahead because many things turn out to be a matter of good or bad fortune anyhow.

14.
a. There are certain people who are just no good.
b. There is some good in everybody.

15.
a. In my case getting what I want has little or nothing to do with luck.
b. Many times we might just as well decide what to do by flipping a coin.

16.
a. Who gets to be the boss often depends on who was lucky enough to be in the right place first.
b. Getting people to do the right thing depends upon ability. Luck has little or nothing to do with it.

17.
a. As far as world affairs are concerned, most of us are the victims of forces we can neither understand, nor control.
b. By taking an active part in political and social affairs the people can control world events.

18.
a. Most people don't realize the extent to which their lives are controlled by accidental happenings.
b. There really is no such thing as "luck."

19.
a. One should always be willing to admit mistakes.
b. It is usually best to cover up one's mistakes.

20.
a. It is hard to know whether or not a person really likes you.
b. How many friends you have depends upon how nice a person you are.

21.
a. In the long run the bad things that happen to us are balanced by the good ones.
b. Most misfortunes are the result of lack of ability, ignorance, laziness, or all three.

22.
a. With enough effort we can wipe out political corruption.
b. It is difficult for people to have much control over the things politicians do in office.

23.
a. Sometimes I can't understand how teachers arrive at the grades they give.
b. There is a direct connection between how hard 1 study and the grades I get.

24.
a. A good leader expects people to decide for themselves what they should do.
b. A good leader makes it clear to everybody what their jobs are.

25.
a. Many times I feel that I have little influence over the things that happen to me.
b. It is impossible for me to believe that chance or luck plays an important role in my life.

(continued)

Table 4.2 Cont.

26.

a. People are lonely because they don't try to be friendly.

b. There's not much use in trying too hard to please people; if they like you, they like you.

27.

a. There is too much emphasis on athletics in high school.

b. Team sports are an excellent way to build character.

28.

a. What happens to me is my own doing.

b. Sometimes I feel that I don't have enough control over the direction my life is taking.

29.

a. Most of the time I can't understand why politicians behave the way they do.

b. In the long run the people are responsible for bad government on a national as well as on a local level.

Score one point for each of the following:
2.a, 3.b, 4.b, 5.b, 6.a, 7.a, 9.a, 10.b, 11.b, 12.b, 13.b, 15.b, 16.a, 17.a, 18.a, 20.a, 21.a, 22.b, 23.a, 25.a, 26.b, 28.b, 29.a.
The higher your score, the greater your external locus of control.
The lower your score, the greater your internal locus of control.

Part 4.7 Breaking up *is* hard to do but might be the healthiest choice

Achieving higher levels of Erikson's psychosocial development, including positive relationships, generally contribute to healthy aging, cognitive and psychological function, and a satisfying life,[44] yet relationships come to an end for many reasons. We may simply grow apart because our interests or perspectives evolve. Or, perhaps we experience the loss of a relationship because of the death of a loved one. And in yet other instances, we might need to terminate a relationship that is not positive and does not contribute to our healthy well-being.

How do we end relationships? There are many ways to end a relationship, either directly or indirectly. As noted earlier, positive relationships involve trust, honesty, reciprocity, and open communication. It should be no surprise that using a more direct approach to ending a relationship (e.g., confrontation) actually results in a more positive outcome.[45] Although it may seem more difficult, it is much better to communicate directly, honestly, and consistently when ending a relationship. Conversely, avoidance and withdrawal (e.g., avoiding contact), or indirect actions, result in more negative or distressful outcomes. So, the initiator of a break-up should employ the same techniques of maintaining a relationship (i.e., open communication) as when ending a relationship.

If the end of the relationship is initiated by someone else, or if there is a loss of the individual, then we will experience feelings of grief and loss. In this case the choice was not ours. Thus, it will be important to engage in coping behaviors that allow us to address the feelings of loss. Grief is the feeling that is associated with loss. We cannot avoid the feeling, but we begin by accepting the painful feelings of loss. Although, it is not possible to predict the amount of time that it will take to move through the grieving process, we do know that people are able to move past the initial intense feelings. Perhaps the only thing that we can do is to stay connected and continue to seek support from other relationships.

Dealing with stress: Relationships as antidotes. We all have the desire to live a rich and full and happy life, and relationships are an essential part of helping us to live a fulfilling life. In fact, in a longitudinal study of older men, researchers reported that relationships are central to quality of life, higher levels of cognitive function, and lower levels of depression.[46] So, the loss of a friendship, a partner, or a relationship will introduce feelings of loneliness and stress. Even if an individual is relatively happy, difficult and stressful situations are a part of everyday life. For example, an argument with a friend, traffic, a basketball game, or relationships at work hold the potential for stress.

The human body has biological and psychological mechanisms for dealing with stress. Cannon coined the phrase **fight of flight** to describe the typical response to a stressful situation. The SNS helps the body to deal with stress by mobilizing the hormones epinephrine and norepinephrine. These hormones help the body cope, but as we indicated earlier, long-term activation of the SNS can have negative consequences.

One way to cope with stress is to engage in relationships. Driven in part by biology, the **tend and befriend** response is almost as common as the fight or flight response.[47] Shelly Taylor found that oxytocin is also released under stress, and this hormone triggers the need for affiliation. So, the elevated levels of the hormone oxytocin result in a need for more social contact which will in turn help to reduce feelings of stress. Although we don't consciously feel the direct effects of increased levels of oxytocin, we increase our social interactions as a way to deal effectively with stressful situations. Effectively dealing with stress involves a physiological response which moves us to seek increased social relations which ultimately helps us to deal with the stressful situation. Social support, or positive relationships and befriending, is essential for health and well-being and ultimately helps us to live longer. It is important to note that these threats to physical and psychological health become even more acute as people age, so relationships become increasingly important for psychological and physical well-being.

A positive, healthy marriage can have literal health benefits to those participating in that union, and that marital happiness certainly influences overall life satisfaction. Compared to people who are never married, divorced, or widowed, people who get married are healthier and they live longer. However, researchers[48] have examined how the extent of marital happiness may influence general happiness, self-reported health, and even one's risk of dying. Since marriage has a positive effect, a buffering hypothesis seems to apply, that is, the union helps individuals cope with the stressors of the world. However, in an unhappy marriage, evidence suggests for an aggravating hypothesis, that is, there is enhanced risk of experiencing poor health. "Compared to individuals who were 'very happily' married, those who were 'not too happy' in marriage were over twice as likely to report worse health and almost 40% more likely to die over the follow-up period..." (p. 1539). An unhappy marriage is undeniably a health risk.

Part 4.8 Relationships as part of my job or career

As the proverbial land of opportunity, the United States is often touted for having what is seen as a reasonable 40-hour work week. Yet many citizens work much more than that each week in order to make ends meet. Ironically, as people's incomes rise, they have less time available for leisure activities – they are too busy working, which is another explanation for the weak connection between earnings and subjective well-being.[49]

Work is an activity that most everyone has to do in order to make a livelihood and much of our daily life is dedicated to what we do for a living. Given that our time commitment to work is probably 40–45 hours, choosing a job that provides satisfaction as well as a salary is probably an important consideration; in fact, more than half our waking life turns out to be dedicated to working.[50] Our goal in this section is not to help you choose a career path but rather to get you to think about what sort of work life you envision for yourself and whether it will be (or already is) a source of enrichment for you.

Industrial-organizational or I/O psychologists study human behavior in the workplace and within organizations of various types. They are often interested in issues of employee motivation and satisfaction, improving job performance, selecting the right applicant for the appropriate position, helping workplaces to become more diverse, and recommending ways for companies to promote a healthy balance for employees between their work and their lives outside of it.

Some I/O psychologists draw distinction between a job and a calling, and it turns out that most workers view their jobs in one of three ways.[51,52] Which of the following fits how you regard the work you do (if you are currently employed) or the work you anticipate doing in a full-time capacity in the future?

- A *job.* Income is necessary in order to purchase food, goods, and services, and to allow an individual and his or her family to survive. To people who are members of this first group, work is seen as something to be done in exchange for pay. Work can usually be left in the workplace – that is, people with jobs don't usually bring work home with them or think about it at all when they are not working. It's not really an important part of their identities.
- A *career.* Work as part of a career allows individuals to pursue achievements, to compete with others in the workplace, and to raise their status or their prestige. Personal pride matters very much to the people who actively advance their careers in this second group. Work is often brought home

by the career-oriented people and, in fact, a large part of career success is doing whatever work needs to be done when it needs to be done. The work is a part of the person's identity in so far as it contributes to the trappings of success and achievement (e.g., high salary and benefits, recognition in the workplace, a large office, perhaps an assistant or secretary, and so on).

- A *calling*. Members of the third group see work as a way to be personally fulfilled and to serve a greater social purpose. Work, then, becomes a form of service to the self and to others, really, a commitment to the larger community. Clearly, work is an important part of the identities of people who see what they do as a calling. A calling can also provide some of the earmarks of success associated with a career, but such things are not the reason people choose to follow a calling. They do so because most cannot imagine doing anything else because the work is meaningful, enjoyable, and it contributes to the greater good. Some people who have followed their calling will even joke that they would do the work for free because they enjoy it so much and find it so personally rewarding (indeed, many devote considerable time to their work even when they are not compensated for it).

Now that you know the three types of workers, where do you see yourself? Researchers suggest that about a third of workers fall into each of the three categories.[53] Is work something to be done to pay the bills and to provide security, or is it much more than that? Does it provide meaning and perhaps enable you to be generative? When work is a calling (or, as some refer to it, a vocation), responsibilities or duties become linked to keen interest or even passion. Individuals who see their work as a calling experience higher levels of satisfaction in the workplace and greater overall life satisfaction than those who refer to their work as just a job or a career.[54] Interestingly, people who believe they are following a calling admit that they find more satisfaction in their work time than their leisure time – work is defining and very positive. Those who have a job feel more satisfaction associated with their out-of-work activities, such as their personal relationships (friends, family) or their hobbies.[55]

Of course, finding a calling is not the only thing about work that is important. Locating work in a positive work environment is also important, as it will affect your well-being and your satisfaction with what you do each work day. In Table 4.3 we present ten qualities that promote engagement and satisfaction with work. This list can be used to evaluate your current or future work environments.

Part 4.9 Putting it all together: Relationships and happiness

What we also know is that happiness is positively linked to career success.[56] Happier people tend to earn higher salaries, demonstrate better work efforts, and receive higher performance evaluations than their less happy counterparts. So, positive emotions influence workplace successes.[57] Indeed, happiness can even

Table 4.3 Ten qualities found in positive work environments[58]

Opportunity for personal control – Workers have some degree of freedom, autonomy, and self-determination in their jobs, and they take part in the organization's decision making. Being able to make decisions, meet goals, and contribute to parts of the job allows people to feel competent.

Opportunity to use skills – Individuals' skills and talents are encouraged and used in the job.

Appropriate, external goals – Employees' satisfaction is linked with moderately strong and concrete goals that enhance a challenging work setting.

Variety – People like to develop new skills on the job, which helps to stimulate their curiosity as well as personal growth.

Clarity in the work environment – Employees routinely receive understandable communications regarding assignments, tasks, responsibilities, concerns, and goals within the workplace.

Availability of money – Some job satisfaction is linked to the amount one is paid, but an equally important factor is the belief that compensation is fair with respect to similar work performed by others.

Physical security – Work setting is pleasant and safe, and that any equipment is designed to promote comfort and reduce the chances of stress or injury.

Supporting supervision – Management is supportive and the organization's leadership is effective.

Opportunity for interpersonal contact – Positive relations exist among coworkers, who provide support, validation, recognition, collegiality, and other social rewards.

Work is valued by the larger society – People want to feel that the work they do contributes to the larger good in some way, that their work makes a difference in the lives of other people.

---

precede career success, so considering how to approach your work with positive attitudes and emotions can lead to workplace success. Happier marriages are linked to happier, more satisfying lives, but negative, toxic marital relationships harm both our ability to be happy and our physical health.

We began this section by providing a context for the importance of staying connected as a fundamental need that is grounded in our evolutionary growth. Similarly, we end this section with the assertion that relationships will continue to be important for our long-term viability as a species. The most important point is that we need to stay connected in healthy relationships that will allow us to thrive.

Notes

1 LeDoux, J. E., Berntson, G. G., Sarter, M., Cacioppo, J. T., Lang, P., ... & Irwin, W. (2002). Basic processes. In J. T. Cacioppo, G. G. Berntson, R. Adolphs, C. S. Carter, R. J. Davidson, McClintock, M.... S. E. Taylor (Eds.), *Foundations in social neuroscience* (pp. 389–490). MIT Press.
2 Bronfenbrenner, U. (1986). Ecology of the family as a context for human development: Research perspectives. *Developmental Psychology, 22,* 723–742.

3 Bronfenbrenner, U., & Ceci, S. J. (1994). Nature-nurture reconceptualized in developmental perspective: A bioecological model. *Psychological Review*, *101*, 568–586.

4 Diener, E. (2012). New findings and future directions for subjective well-being research. *American Psychologist*, *67*(8), 591–597. https://doi.org/10.1037/a0029541

5 MacDonald, G., & Leary, M. R. (2005). Why does social exclusion hurt? The relationship between social and physical pain. *Psychological Bulletin*, *131*, 202–223.

6 DeWall, C. N., & Bushman, B. J. (2011). Social acceptance and rejection: The sweet and the bitter. *Current Directions in Psychological Science*, *20*(4), 256–260. https://doi.org/10.1177/0963721411417545

7 MacDonald, G., & Leary, M. R. (2005). Why does social exclusion hurt? The relationship between social and physical pain. *Psychological Bulletin*, *131*, 202–223.

8 DeWall, C. N., & Bushman, B. J. (2011). Social acceptance and rejection: The sweet and the bitter. *Current Directions in Psychological Science*, *20*(4), 256–260. https://doi.org/10.1177/0963721411417545.

9 MacDonald, G., & Leary, M. R. (2005). Why does social exclusion hurt? The relationship between social and physical pain. *Psychological Bulletin*, *131*, 202–223.

10 Diener, E., & Seligman, M. E. P. (2002). Very happy people. *Psychological Science*, *13*, 81–84.

11 Diener, E., & Seligman, M. E. P. (2004). Beyond money: Toward and economy of well-being. *Psychological Science in the Public Interest*, *5*, 1–31.

12 Diener, E., & Biswas-Diener, R. (2008). *Happiness: Unlocking the mysteries of psychological wealth*. Blackwell Publishing.

13 Peplau, L. A., & Perlman, D. (1982). Perspectives on loneliness. In L. A. Peplau & D. Perman (Eds.), *Loneliness: A sourcebook of current theory, research and therapy* (pp. 1–8). Wiley.

14 Hawkley, L. C., & Cacioppo. J. T. (2010). Loneliness matters: A theoretical and empirical review of consequences and mechanisms. *Annals of Behavioral Medicine*, *40*, 218–227.

15 Jaremka, L. M., Andridge, R. R., Fagundes, C. P., Alfano, C. M., Povoski, S. P., Lipari, A. M., … & Kiecolt-Glaser, J. K. (2014). Pain, depression, and fatigue: Loneliness as a longitudinal risk factor. *Health Psychology*, *33*(9), 948–957. https://doi.org/10.1037/a0034012

16 Cacioppo, S., Grippo, A. J., London, S., Goossens, L., & Cacioppo, J. T. (2015). Loneliness: Clinical important interventions. *Perspectives on Psychological Science*, *10*, 238–249.

17 Costa, P. T., & McCrae, R. R. (1995). Primary traits of Eysenck's P-E-N system: Three- and five-factor solutions. *Journal of Personality and Social Psychology*, *69*, 308–317.

18 Costa, P. T., & McCrae, R. R. (2009). The five-factor model and the NEO inventories. In J. N. Butcher (Ed.), *Oxford handbook of personality assessment* (pp. 299–322). Oxford University Press.

19 Roccas, S., Sagiv, L., Schwartz, S. H., & Knafo, A. (2002). The Big Five personality factors and personal values. *Personality and Social Psychology Bulletin*, *28*(6), 789–801. https://doi.org/10.1177/0146167202289008

20 Eysenck, H. J. (1992). Four ways five factors are not basic. *Personality and Individual Differences*, *13*, 667–673.

21 DeWall, C. N., & Bushman, B. J. (2011). Social acceptance and rejection: The sweet and the bitter. *Current Directions in Psychological Science*, *20*(4), 256–260. https://doi.org/10.1177/0963721411417545.

22 Damiano, C. R., Mazefsky, C. A., White, S. W., & Dichter, G. S. (2014). Future directions for research in autism spectrum disorders. *Journal of Clinical Child & Adolescent Psychology, 43*(5), 828–848. https://doi.org/10.1080/15374416.2014.945214

23 Kopp, N., Climer, S., & Dougherty, J. D. (2015). Moving from capstones toward cornerstones: Successes and challenges in applying systems biology to identify mechanisms of autism spectrum disorders. *Frontiers in Genetics, 6*, 1–16. https://doi.org/10.3389/fgene.2015.00301

24 Harlow H. F., Dodsworth R. O., & Harlow M. K. (1965). Total social isolation in monkeys. *Proceedings of the National Academy of Sciences of the United States of America.* www.ncbi.nlm.nih.gov/pmc/articles/PMC285801/pdf/pnas00159-0105.pdf

25 Stayton, D. J., & Ainsworth, M. D. (1973). Individual differences in infant responses to brief, everyday separations as related to other infant and maternal behaviors. *Developmental Psychology, 9*, 226–235.

26 Ainsworth, M. S. (1989). Attachments beyond infancy. *American Psychologist, 44*, 709–716.

27 Birnbaum, G. E., Reis, H. T., Mikulincer, M., Gillath, O., & Orpaz, A. (2006). When sex is more than just sex: Attachment orientations, sexual experience, and relationship quality. *Journal of Personality and Social Psychology, 91*, 929–943.

28 Erikson, E. H. (1974). *Dimensions of a new identity.* Jefferson Lectures in the Humanities. W.W. Norton.

29 Premack, D., & Woodruff, G. (1978). Does the chimpanzee have a theory of mind? *Behavioral and Brain Sciences, 1*, 515–526.

30 Hartup, W. W., & Stevens, N. (1999). Friendships and adaptation across the life span. *Current Directions in Psychological Science, 8*, 76–79.

31 Nisbett, R. E., & Wilson, T. D. (1977). The halo effect: Evidence for unconscious alteration of judgments. *Journal of Personality and Social Psychology, 35*(4), 250–256. https://doi.org/10.1037/0022-3514.35.4.250

32 Stephen, I. D., Hiew, V., Coetzee, V., Tiddeman, B. P., & Perrett, D. I. (2017). Facial shape analysis identifies valid cues to aspects of physiological health in Caucasian, Asian, and African populations. *Frontiers in Psychology, 8*, Article 1883. https://doi.org/10.3389/fpsyg.2017.01883

33 Myers, D. G. (2013). Sexual orientation, marriage, and students of faith. In D. S. Dunn, R. A. R. Gurung, K. Z. Naufel, & J. H. Wilson (Eds.), *Controversy in the classroom: Using hot topics to foster critical thinking* (pp. 81–104). American Psychological Association.

34 Nilakantan, A., Younger, J., Aron, A., & Mackey, S. (2014). Preoccupation in an early-romantic relationship predicts experimental pain relief. *Pain Medicine, 15*(6), 947–953. https://doi.org/10.1111/pme.12422

35 Alsup, S., Weisbaum, E., Vogel, T., & Siegel, D. J. (2020). Family relations, friendships, and love. In W. W. IsHak (Ed.), *The handbook of wellness medicine* (pp. 553–564). Cambridge University Press. https://doi.org/10.1017/9781108650182.047

36 Jaremka, L. M., Andridge, R. R., Fagundes, C. P., Alfano, C. M., Povoski, S. P., Lipari, A. M., … & Kiecolt-Glaser, J. K. (2014). Pain, depression, and fatigue: Loneliness as a longitudinal risk factor. *Health Psychology, 33*(9), 948–957. https://doi.org/10.1037/a0034012

37 Miller, A. G., & Rorer, L. G. (1982). Toward an understanding of the fundamental attribution error: Essay diagnosticity in the attitude attribution

paradigm. *Journal of Research in Personality, 16*(1), 41–59. https://doi.org/10.1016/0092-6566(82)90039-3

38 Harvey, J. H., & Omarzu, J. (1997). Minding the close relationship. *Personality and Social Psychology Review, 1,* 224–240.

39 Hackenbracht, J., & Gasper, K. (2013). I'm all ears: The need to belong motivates listening to emotional disclosure. *Journal of Experimental Social Psychology, 49,* 915–921.

40 Sprecher, S., Treger, S., Wondra, J. D., Hilaire, N., & Wallpe, K. (2013). Taking turns: Reciprocal self-disclosure promotes liking in initial interactions. *Journal of Experimental Social Psychology, 49,* 860–866.

41 Kim, J., Joseph, S., & Price, S. (2020). The positive psychology of relational depth and its association with unconditional positive self-regard and authenticity. *Person-Centered and Experiential Psychotherapies*. Advance online publication. https://doi.org/10.1080/14779757.2020.1717983

42 Grossman, I., & Koss, E. (2014). Exploring Solomon's paradox: Self-distancing eliminates the self-other asymmetry in wise reasoning about close relationships in younger and older adults. *Psychological Science, 25,* 1571–1580.

43 Rotter, J. B. (1966). Generalized expectancies for internal versus external locus of control. *Psychological Monograph: General and Applied, 80,* 1–28.

44 Malone, J. C., Liu, S. R., Vaillant, G. E., Rentz, D. M., & Waldinger, R. J. (2016). Midlife Eriksonian psychosocial development: Setting the stage for late-life cognitive and emotional health. *Developmental Psychology, 52*(3), 496–508. https://doi.org/10.1037/a0039875

45 Collins, T. J., & Gillath, O. (2012). Attachment, breakup strategies, and associated outcomes: The effects of security enhancement on the selection of breakup strategies. *Journal of Research in Personality, 46,* 210–222.

46 Malone, J. C., Liu, S. R., Vaillant, G. E., Rentz, D. M., & Waldinger, R. J. (2016). Midlife Eriksonian psychosocial development: Setting the stage for late-life cognitive and emotional health. *Developmental Psychology, 52*(3), 496–508. https://doi.org/10.1037/a0039875

47 Taylor, S. E. (2006). Tend and befriend: Biobehavioral bases of affiliation under stress. *Current Directions in Psychological Science, 15,* 273–277.

48 Lawrence, E. M., Rogers, R. G., & Zajacova, A. (2018). Marital happiness, marital status, health, and longevity. *Journal of Happiness Studies, 20,* 1539–1561. https://doi.org/10.1007/s10902-018-0009-9

49 Kahneman, D., Krueger, A. B., Schkade, D., Schwartz, N., & Stone, A. A. (2006). Would you be happier if you were richer? A focusing illusion. *Science, 312,* 1908–1910.

50 Wrzesniewski, A., McCauley, C., Rozin, P., & Schwartz, B. (1997). Jobs, careers, and callings: People's relations to their work. *Journal of Research in Personality, 31,* 21–33.

51 Wrzesniewski et al. (1997).

52 Wrzesniewski, A. (2012). Callings in work. In K. S. Cameron & G. M. Spreitzer (Eds.), *The Oxford handbook of positive organizational scholarship* (pp. 45–55). Oxford University Press.

53 Wrzesniewski, A., McCauley, C., Rozin, P., & Schwartz, B. (1997). Jobs, careers, and callings: People's relations to their work. *Journal of Research in Personality, 31,* 21–33.

54 Wrzesniewski et al. (1997).

55 Wrzesniewski, A., Rozin, P., & Bennett, G. (2003). Working, playing, and eating: Making the most of most moments. In C. L. M. Keyes & J. Haidt (Eds.), *Flourishing:*

Positive psychology and the life well-lived (pp. 185–204). American Psychological Association.

56 Walsh, L. C., Boehm, J. K., & Lyubomirsky, S. (2018). Does happiness promote career success? Revisiting the evidence. *Journal of Career Assessment, 26*(2), 199–219. https://doi.org/10.1177/1069072717751441

57 Diener, E., Thapa, S., & Tay, L. (2020). Positive emotions at work. *Annual Review of Organizational Psychology and Organizational Behavior, 7,* 451–477. http://doi.org/10/1146/annurev-orgpsych-02119-044908

58 Warr, P. (1999). Well-being in the workplace. In D. Kahneman, E. Diener, & N. Schwartz (Eds.), *Well-being: The foundations of hedonic psychology* (pp. 392–412). Russell Sage.

Section 5   In closing
My happiness

In some ways, everything in this book – all of the preceding sections – were related to happiness, overall life satisfaction, or what psychological scientists might precisely label as "subject well-being." As you might imagine, there is quite a bit of research and scholarship available about happiness, and many of the relationships between happiness and health and wealth have been presented in previous sections. What are the benefits of happiness? Happier people live longer, experience fewer illnesses, remain married longer, are more creative, earn more money, are more helpful to others, and tend to work harder and better in their professions.

Two main takeaways that prominent happiness researchers[1] would want us to know are that (1) happiness is a process, not a place, and (2) happiness more than feels good; it is good for you (i.e., it is to be used *and* enjoyed).

Part 5.1 Subjective well-being and why it matters

For most people, happiness is a present state of being, one based in emotion, as in "I am happy" or "I feel pretty happy." Good feelings are associated with a moment in time – how individuals feel about their world and their place in it. This approach makes sense because when a peer asks us, "How are you doing?", we reflect on how we feel right then and there. We are less likely to think about how happy we are in the big picture of our lives, which might require more reflection and a more detailed answer than our friend's polite inquiry was actually after.

In contrast, psychologists are usually interested in a broader view of people's happiness, and they often refer to measuring people's **subjective well-being**. "Subjective" is the key word because it implies that self-reports about people's states are personal, slanted by their experience and perspective, and open to very little independent verification. I know how I feel but I can only guess how a friend or a stranger is feeling. Subjective well-being and the variety of psychological measures used to assess it point to what are known as **individual differences** in psychology, that is, people's responses to them vary. For our purposes, some people report higher subjective well-being than others, though most people do report being relatively happy.[2,3,4] Indeed, people may report being above the neutral point of happiness but they may not be satisfied with

DOI: 10.4324/9781003188711-6

Table 5.1 The satisfaction with life scale[52]

Here are five statements with which you may agree or disagree. Using the scale provided, indicate your agreement with each item by placing the appropriate number on the line preceding that item. Please be open and honest in your responses.						
1	2	3	4	5	6	7
strongly disagree	*disagree*	*slightly disagree*	*neither agree nor disagree*	*slightly agree*	*agree*	*strongly agree*

_____ 1. In most ways my life is close to ideal.
_____ 2. The conditions of my life are excellent.
_____ 3. I am satisfied with my life.
_____ 4. So far I have gotten the important things I want in life.
_____ 5. If I could live my life over, I would change almost nothing.

To obtain your total score, which can range from 5 to 35, add up your answers to the five questions. Scores above the midpoint of 20 suggest satisfaction with life. If you want to characterize your particular score, use these ranges: 31–35 = extremely satisfied, 26–30 = satisfied, 21–25 = slightly satisfied, 20 = neutral, 15–19=slightly dissatisfied, 10–14 = dissatisfied, and 5–9 = extremely dissatisfied.

their lives, that is, their personal and societal situations.[5] To be very happy, you need both very desirable personal circumstances and to live in an affluent, contented culture with close, reliable ties with other people.[6]

Subjective well-being has three elements: How happy we say we are, our general satisfaction with our lives as they are lived, and how neurotic or anxious we tend to feel day to day. People with high levels of subjective well-being say they are quite happy, are not very anxious (low neuroticism), and are very satisfied with their lives. Life satisfaction is often used as a way to gauge happiness and well-being. As a self-assessment, it is more of a global judgment, one weighing how well people believe their lives are compared to how they could be. Before you continue reading, why not assess how satisfied you are with your life by completing the short set of questions in Table 5.1?

Interpreting your score:[7]

Extremely satisfied. You feel that your life has gone very well, and the circumstances of your life are excellent. Most people who score in this range feel that the major areas of their lives are positive: Work, leisure, relationships, and health. They don't feel that their lives are perfect, but that their lives are very rewarding.

Satisfied. Your life is rewarding, but you would like to see improvement in some areas. People in this range are happy and feel very good about their lives.

Slightly satisfied. You feel that generally your life is going well, although you would like to see improvement in some domains. Some areas of your life need improvement, or most areas are going modestly well, but you have not yet achieved the level you would like to attain in many areas.

Neutral. There is a mix of good and bad in your life. There are about as
many things going well as things you would like to improve. Things
are not terrible, but neither are they as rewarding as you would like.

Slightly dissatisfied. If your score on life satisfaction has dropped recently
due to specific bad events, then a score in this range is not of concern.
However, if your score is chronically in the somewhat low range, you
might want to ask why, and what you can do to increase your satisfaction. Perhaps there are things in your life that cannot be changed
at this point but in this case, should you change your expectations?
Perhaps there are conditions that you can change? If your life is on
tan upward trajectory and you are optimistic about the future, there
is probably no concern.

Dissatisfied. Life satisfaction score in this low range can be a matter of
concern, and you should think about how to improve things. Would
seeing a clergyperson or mental health professional help? Perhaps you
are just going through a temporary bad time or have not achieved
many of the things you hope to do, in which case your score might
not be of concern. However, in other cases, scores in this range point
to some areas of your life needing strong improvement.

Extremely dissatisfied. Perhaps some recent extremely bad event has
influenced your current life satisfaction. However, if your life satisfaction has been in the low range for some time, some things in your
life are in need of change and you might need the help of others,
including professionals, to improve your situation. A number of
things may be drastically wrong, and it is time to make very serious
efforts to turn your life around.

What is your score on the *Satisfaction with life scale*? Does it indicate you are
satisfied or even quite satisfied with your daily existence? Or are you less satisfied with how your life is going these days? People with the highest levels of
life satisfaction feel that their life circumstances are great. They tend to view
the major areas of their lives – relationships, physical and mental health, work
or career, and leisure – in very positive terms. Such satisfaction does not mean
that life is perfect or grand, rather, that it usually provides rewarding, beneficial experiences (you have good friends you can call to chat or make plans, you
look forward to getting to the office each day, when you think of your family
you feel warm and lucky). At the other extreme, very low levels of life satisfaction point to the need for change, that things are not going well in most major
areas of daily life (work is a drudgery, you feel stressed all the time, things are
not going well with your significant other), that help – likely professional psychological help – is sorely needed.[8]

Where leading an enriched life is concerned, people who are very satisfied
with their lives enjoy close and strong bonds with their families and friends,
and perhaps also a rewarding relationship with a romantic partner. They view
their lives as meaningful and possess goals and values that motivate them.
Familiar addictions, including alcohol, drugs, or gambling are rarely an issue

for those who report being high in life satisfaction.[9] The good news for folks who are satisfied with their lives is that they are likely to remain at relatively steady levels of satisfaction and happiness.[10,11] Most of us tend to "float" around our own average levels of happiness and life satisfaction, sometimes we rise a little higher, other times we fall a tad below our usual baseline.

What causes these ups and downs? To understand that, we will explore what factors in daily experience do – or do not – increase our happiness. If we know what is likely to increase our happiness, then we can choose to do things that are likely to enrich our lives while avoiding those things that have little impact on whether we feel good or contented.

Part 5.2 What makes people happy?

To understand what factors influence our happiness, envision your own happiness as a pie (choose your favorite kind of pie, whether it's apple, coconut crème, or lemon meringue). Imagine cutting the pie down the middle. One half of the pie (a full 50%) represents genetic contributions to our happiness; many of us are happier than others we encounter, others less so. This part of the pie cannot really be changed – think of it as your preordained or inherited level of happiness, coupled with elements of your personality that remain relatively stable across time.[12]

What about the rest of the pie? A slice representing 10% represents the environment we inhabit and the things in it that affect how happy we are. This slice – let's call it your life circumstances – can't really be altered, either. You didn't select your situation – your family, your nation, the city or town or countryside where you grew up – those qualities were just there for you.[13] Their nature and presence had – and still has – some influence on your subjective well-being.

The last third of the pie, which amounts to 40%, is the sweet spot: This sizeable slice is what psychologist Sonja Lyubomirsky calls *intentional actions* or steps we can take to make ourselves happier.[14] In essence – and this is important – it is theoretically possible for people to enhance their own happiness by choosing to act with intent.[15] Such steps include behaviors like making new friends, getting physical exercise, volunteering to help others, choosing work that is both meaningful and rewarding, traveling, and so forth. Taking concrete steps can promote subjective well-being and incrementally increase our feelings of happiness.[16] Now, Lyubomirsky is clear that any such boost in happiness is not going to be a dramatic one; if you are a hypothetical 5 on a 10-point happiness scale, running a triathlon is not going to turn you into a 9. However, moving upwards to a 6 or even a 7 by exercising choice and control over what you do (including the triathlon) is both possible and beneficial, so you will feel happier in your world.[17] If nothing else, you will be much better off than where you started.

Now that we know that intentional actions can potentially alter our happiness, we can explore what sort of behaviors will enhance our happiness or have little or no effect. Let's focus on those factors that do *not* promote happiness first.

First, it turns out that self-reported happiness does not vary that much with age. Some people expect that being young is associated with greater happiness – you have your whole life ahead of you, after all – so it must follow that being old is linked to lower happiness because older people know their time is limited. Not so. Happiness does not vary much with age.[18] If anything, it may be best characterized by a "U"-shaped connection between years of age and happiness. Young adults (20s and 30s) report relatively high happiness, which is reduced in middle age (40s and 50s), only to rise again for older adults (60s and 70s).[19] And, in any case, age is not something we can change.

What are some of the other nonstarters where happiness is concerned? Well, although being physically attractive can help in other venues of life (say, during a job interview), good-looking people are not happier than those folks who are less attractive.[20,21] The same is true of intelligence and acquired education, as neither seems to have an impact of how satisfied people are with their lives.[22] More education might improve your income, but a degree or even multiple degrees will not necessarily make you happier. Being happy is not dependent on gender, either; despite the social advantages men sometimes enjoy over women (such as higher salaries[23]), men and women report similar levels of happiness.[24] Even being a parent does not inflate happiness, presumably because the joys and challenges of raising children cancel one another out.[25] That's right: Having children is not a way to become happier. Indeed, despite what many people believe, people who have kids are not happier than those who do not.

What factors are linked with happiness? We will consider moderate predictors of happiness first. Although being physically healthy has a modest connection to happiness, keep in mind that people are surprisingly malleable, which means they can adjust to health problems.[26] A better way to look at this relationship is that happiness might promote better health, particularly because there is a positive connection between self-reported happiness and people's longevity.[27] Maintaining good health is certainly something you can do, notably by getting enough sleep, exercising regularly, eating healthy meals, avoiding smoking, not drinking alcohol to excess, and so on. None of this is apt to be surprising, of course, but enacting these sorts of healthy behaviors is a good way to enrich your life. Yet for many people maintaining them is a challenge. Still, there is some evidence that subjective well-being can improve self-reported physical health[28] and health-related behaviors (exercising, not smoking).[29]

Good interpersonal relations – having friends to talk to and to rely on – is linked with higher levels of happiness.[30,31] Social activity is important, clearly representing an area where choices (hosting friends, going out with them to concerts or sporting events) pay happiness dividends. Now, those 357 *Facebook* friends you have don't count here; rather, we are focusing on your really important close relationships, like the ones discussed earlier in this book.

People who are spiritual or actively and sincerely religious also tend to be happier than nonreligious individuals.[32] The relationship is likely to be more complex than it appears, and it's likely to be dependent on the level of affluence a given country enjoys. Thus, in nations where resources are strained or even limited, people seem to take greater solace in and benefit from religion. In those countries where material wealth is sufficient (think the United

States and other Western nations), organized religion plays less of a role in day-to-day happiness because circumstances are generally good.[33]

What are the strongest predictors of happiness? Aside from the afore-mentioned genetic predispositions (half of your happiness pie), only a few factors stand out. First is marriage or being in a happy marital relationship. Some research suggests that married people are happier than either single or divorced people,[34] just as higher levels of life satisfaction with marriage is linked to higher well-being,[35] though the association appears to be a small one.[36] However, other research suggests that single people are not less happy than those who are married.[37,38,39] More research is needed to clarify these disparate perspectives. A better way to think about this issue is whether and how satisfied people are with their close, romantic relationships.

What about your worklife? Well, work both fills and provides structure to our days, so perhaps it makes some sense that job satisfaction is tied to people's general sense of being happy.[40] Other researchers point to unemployment as a factor that lowers people's life satisfaction.[41] The connection is not a simple one, as we can imagine that liking one's job can lead to higher levels of happiness, just as being happy, in turn, can likely lead people to like their work more. What are the characteristics of the best places to work? What are the general indicators of good workplaces? When researchers[42] generate evidence-informed answers to these important questions, the following characteristics emerge as being positively related to workplace happiness:

- Opportunities for personal control and maximum possible flexibility positions with a variety of tasks.
- Supportive supervisors and managers, providing just the right amount of feedback.
- Respect and status, which should lead to feelings of competence and pride.
- Good pay with fringe benefits.
- Clear job performance expectations.

People who are happy and engaged in their work are better workers. People who are happy tend to have more friends and closer friends. People who are happy tend to have, on average, better health and they tend to live longer. Happier people tend to be more trusting and tend to help others more. Finally, happier people tend to be more peaceful and they cooperate more often.[43] That does sound like a more enjoyable work environment!

What's left? We noted at the outset of our discussion of subjective well-being that higher levels of neuroticism, a personality trait representing anxiety and insecurity, is associated with lower levels of subjective well-being. The trait of *extraversion*, which is marked by outgoing, gregarious, and sociable behavior, is a solid predictor of happiness.[44] Extraverts are fun to be around, as they can be the life of the party and naturally draw others to them. Extraverts also exhibit a bit of what we can call a favorability bias because they are apt to see their lives as being more positive than they probably are – this is effectively a psychologically protective shield – just as individuals who are high in neuroticism will see their world as being darker and more negative than may be warranted.[45]

Part 5.3 Can we manufacture happiness?

It's pretty obvious that happiness is a desirable state or outcome, and though some of the factors that determine happiness may be outside of our direct control, we are able to influence some of those factors. Can we actually manufacture our own happiness, and order it up like we would from DoorDash or UberEats? Let's think about two different types of examples within this realm.

When a weekend is like a vacation. On the basis of the latest data, we can decipher that U.S. workers are time poor. There is no legally mandated vacation in the United States, which leaves it the only industrialized nation without such a policy. When workers are allotted vacation days, they tend not to take those days as compared (proportionally) to European employees, even though there is clear evidence that not utilizing vacation time is related to lower happiness. These researchers[46] set out to replicate previous work in the area of the psychological hack of "if you are not going to take your vacation, then treating the weekend like a vacation can have similar happiness benefits to vacation-taking."

Just to be clear, the benefits of taking vacations are well-known; there is documented evidence that vacations lead to increases in health, being creative, performance in one's job, happiness levels, and overall life satisfaction. If the benefit of "taking a break" via a vacation has all of those health benefits, these researchers wanted to continue to explore the notion of "taking a mini-break" over the course of a two-day weekend? Can similar health and happiness benefits be realized compared to those that are known from vacation-taking? Across three studies, researchers concluded that when the weekend is truly treated like a two-day vacation, people experience a happiness boost on the Monday that they return to work. The researchers are careful not to make claims of causality (as they should be), but during the mini-vacation weekend, individuals focused on the present, minimized time on chores such as housework, and reported increased levels of happiness.[47] Even if you can't get away for a vacation, there are clear benefits to getting away for a weekend.

Does "retail therapy" actually lead to happiness? Some people have believed that retail therapy is a bad approach to dealing with sadness because these behaviors seem to imply a lack of behavior control/higher impulsivity. Is that the case, and is there a postevent "regret phase" following retail therapy? Researchers[48] studied these ideas and discovered that bad moods do prompt retail therapy episodes, but these events, although perhaps unplanned, can also be strategically motivated and do lead to improved/enhanced moods, and this improved mood can last over time. Considering retail therapy from a slightly different yet related perspective, if the presumption is that sadness is caused by forces outside of a person's control, then the act of going shopping is a behavior that is within a person's control, is it this countermanding or cancelling of out-of-control versus in-control behaviors which leads to the pleasurable outcome that shopping restores happiness? Different researchers[49] actually tested that notion experimentally, and they determined over three studies that purchase decisions (i.e., retail therapy) allowed for the restoration of personal control and reduction of sadness levels.

The notion of retail therapy to reduce sadness/negative moods has been confirmed by other researchers as well.[50] In fact, these researchers went so far as to develop a retail therapy scale, in which they refined and identified four factors or themes: (1) therapeutic shopping motivations, (2) positive mood aspects of therapeutic shopping, (3) negative mood aspects of therapeutic shopping, and (4) therapeutic shopping. [Therapeutic shopping is the researcher's fancy method for saying "retail therapy"]. The items were all answered on a scale from 1 = *strongly disagree* to 5 = *strongly agree*. Table 5.2 presents the items on the subscales described here. ERIC–there are no directions for calculating the Retail Therapy subscales–the directions need to be included for the reader or the whole table and some of the discussion needs to be deleted.-Dana

Table 5.2 Retail therapy scale[53]

Using the scale provided, indicate your degree of disagreement or agreement with each of the items presented.

1	2	3	4	5
strongly disagree	disagree	neither disagree or agree	agree	strongly agree

Therapeutic shopping motivation
_____ I shop to relieve my stress.
_____ I shop to cheer myself up.
_____ I shop to make myself feel better.
_____ I shop to compensate for a bad day.
_____ I shop to feel relaxed.
_____ I shop to feel good about myself.

Positive mood reinforcement: Therapeutic shopping value
_____ Shopping is a positive reaction.
_____ Shopping gives me a sense of achievement.
_____ I like the visual stimulation shopping provides.
_____ Shopping provides me with knowledge of new styles.
_____ I enjoy being in a pleasant environment that shopping provides.
_____ Finding a great deal reinforces positive feelings about myself.

Negative mood reinforcement: Therapeutic shopping value
_____ Shopping is an escape from loneliness.
_____ Shopping is a way to remove myself from stressful environments.
_____ Shopping is a way to take my mind off things that are bothering me.
_____ Shopping for something new fills an empty feeling.
_____ Shopping is a way to control things when other things seem out of control.

Therapeutic shopping outcome
_____ My shopping trip to relieve my bad mood is successful.
_____ After a shopping trip to make myself feel better, the good feelings generated last at least for the rest of the day.
_____ I feel good immediately after my shopping trip to relieve a bad mood.
_____ I use items I bought during my shopping to relieve a bad mood.
_____ When I use items I bought during my shopping to relieve my bad mood, I remember the shopping experience.

Part 5.4 Health leads to happiness; can happiness "cause" health?

As it turns out, this is an important and fairly interesting question! It has been confirmed through correlational, longitudinal, and experimental means that happier people are healthier than nonhappy people, but what is the precise relationship between happiness and health? We know that

↑health leads to ↑happiness

but it is also the case that

↑happiness leads to ↑health

In other words, do increases in happiness actually lead to improvements in health? Just because the first statistical relationship is true does not mean the second statistical relationship is also true.

What these researchers[51] strived to determine was, given that we have some evidence that happiness is linked to improvements in health, is that linkage causal, that is, if a person were to actively seek to become happier, would that directly lead to measurable improvements in health? They cleverly performed a six-month randomized control trial study with community adults with a treatment and control group and examined subjective well-being, self-reported physical health, and a number of other outcome measures, and they concluded from the accumulation of evidence that the causal link was present – happiness does lead to better health. From this evidence, it is clear that happier individuals (as compared to less happy individuals) have improved cardiovascular health, have better immune functioning, participate in healthier behaviors, and live longer. Making the effort to find, discover, and build your own happiness can have tangible benefits ranging far beyond happiness itself.

Part 5.5 Now it's all together

Each of the preceding four sections has ended with a "putting it all together" section, and here at the conclusion of our book, we hope it is all together for you. Your physical health, your mental health, your wealth, and your relationships are challenging and difficult concepts to navigate in today's world, for nearly anyone at nearly any age. We hope we have brought you the best and most useful ideas from psychological science and shown you how to apply them to your daily life. We are passionate about this, as your authors have dedicated all of their professional lives to the teaching of psychology and advancing our collective knowledge of human behavior. Happiness and health are lofty goals to aspire to, but what else could be more important for you and those around you, both locally and globally?

Notes

1 Diener, E., & Biswas-Diener, R. (2008). *Happiness: Unlocking the mysteries of psychological wealth*. Blackwell Publishing.
2 Myers, D. G. (2000). The funds, friends, and faith of happy people. *American Psychologist, 55*(1), 56–67.
3 Myers, D. G., & Diener, E. (1995). Who is happy? *Psychological Science, 6*(1), 10–19.
4 Witters, D. (2011). *Americans happier, less stressed in 2010*. www.gallup.com
5 Diener, E., Diener, C., Choi, H., & Oishi, S. (2018). Revisiting "most people are happy" – and discovering when they are not. *Perspectives on Psychological Science, 13*(2), 166–170. https://doi.org/10.1177/1745691618765111
6 Diener, E., Seligman, M. E. P., Choi, H., & Oishi, S. (2018). Happiest people revisited. *Perspectives on Psychological Science, 13*(2), 176–184. https://doi.org/10.1177/1745691617697077
7 Diener, E., & Biswas-Diener, R. (2008). *Happiness: Unlocking the mysteries of psychological wealth*. Blackwell Publishing.
8 Diener & Biswas-Diener (2008).
9 Diener & Biswas-Diener (2008).
10 Diener, E. (1994). Assessing subjective well-being: Progress and opportunities. *Social Indicators Research, 31*(2), 103–157.
11 McCrae, R. (2011). Personality traits and the potential of positive psychology. In K. M. Sheldon, T. B. Kashdan, & M. F. Steger (Eds.), *Designing positive psychology: Taking stock and moving forward* (pp. 193–206). Oxford University Press.
12 Lyubomirsky, S., Sheldon, K. M., & Schkade, D. (2005). Pursuing happiness: The architecture of sustainable change. *Review of General Psychology, 9*(2), 111–131.
13 Lyubomirsky et al. (2005).
14 Lyubomirsky, S. (2008). *The how of happiness: A scientific approach to getting the life you want*. Penguin.
15 Sheldon, K. M., & Lyubomirsky, S. (2019). Revisiting the Sustainable Happiness Model and pie chart: Can happiness be successfully pursued? *The Journal of Positive Psychology*. Advance online publication. https://doi.org/10.1080/17439760.2019.1689421
16 Lyubomirsky, S., Sheldon, K. M., & Schkade, D. (2005). Pursuing happiness: The architecture of sustainable change. *Review of General Psychology, 9*(2), 111–131.
17 Lyubomirsky, S. (2008). *The how of happiness: A scientific approach to getting the life you want*. Penguin.
18 Cooper, C., Bennington, P., King, M., Jenkins, R., Farrell, M., Brugha, T., … & Livingston, G. (2011). Happiness across age groups: Results from the 2007 National Psychiatric Morbidity Survey. *International Journal of Geriatric Psychiatry, 26*(6), 608–614. doi: 10.1002/gps.2570
19 Stone, A. A., Schwartz, J. E., Broderick, J. E., & Deaton, A. (2010). A snapshot of the age distribution of psychological well-being in the United States. *PNAS: Proceedings of the National Academy of Sciences, 107*, 9985–9990. http://doi.org/10.1073/pnas.1003744107
20 Diener, E., Wolsic, B., & Fugita, F. (1995). Physical attractiveness and subjective well-being. *Journal of Personality and Social Psychology, 6*(1), 120–129.
21 Ross, C. E., & Van Willigen, M. (1997). Education and the subjective quality of life. *Journal of Health & Social Behavior, 38*(3), 275–297.
22 Diener, E., Kesebir, P., & Tov, W. (2009). Happiness. In M. R. Leary & R. H. Hoyle (Eds.), *Handbook of individual differences in social behavior* (pp. 147–160). Guilford.

23 Lykken, D. (1999). *Happiness: The nature and nurture of joy and contentment*. St. Martin's.

24 Myers, D. G. (1992). *The pursuit of happiness: Who is happy – and why*. Morrow.

25 Argyle, M. (2001). *The psychology of happiness* (2nd ed.). Routledge.

26 Riis, J., Loewenstein, G., Baron, J., Jepson, C., Fagerlin, A., & Ubel, P. A. (2005). Ignorance of hedonic adaptation to hemodialysis: A study using ecological momentary assessment. *Journal of Experimental Psychology: General, 134*(1), 3–9.

27 Veenhoven, R. (2008). Healthy happiness: Effects of happiness on physical health and the consequences for preventive care. *Journal of Happiness Studies, 9*(3), 449–469.

28 Kushlev, K., Heintzelman, S. J., Lutes, L. D., Wirtz, D., Kanippayoor, J. M., Leitner, D., & Diener, E. (2020). Does happiness improve health? Evidence from a randomized control trial. *Psychological Science, 31*(7), 807–821. doi: 10.1177/0956797620919673

29 Kushlev, K., Drummond, D. M., & Diener, E. (2020). Subjective well-being and health behaviors in 2.5 million Americans. *Applied Psychology: Health and Well-Being, 12*(1), 166–187. https://doi.org/10.1111/aphw.12178

30 Diener, E., & Seligman, M. E. P. (2002). Very happy people. *Psychological Science, 13*(1), 80–83.

31 Diener, E., & Seligman, M. E. P. (2004). Beyond money: Toward an economy of well-being. *Psychological Science in the Public Interest, 5*(1), 1–31.

32 Myers, D. G. (2008). Religion and human flourishing. In M. Eid & R. J. Larsen (Eds.), *The science of subjective well-being* (pp. 323–346). Guilford.

33 Diener, E., Tay, L., & Myers, D. G. (2011). The religion paradox: If religion makes people happy, why are so many dropping out? *Journal of Personality and Social Psychology, 101*(6), 1278–1290. https://doi.org/10.1037/a00224402

34 Myers, D. G., & Diener, E. (1995). Who is happy? *Psychological Science, 6*(1), 10–19.

35 Proulx, C. M., Helms, H. M., & Buehler, B. (2007). Marital quality and personal well-being: A meta-analysis. *Journal of Marriage and Family, 69*(3), 576–593.

36 Jebb, A. T., Morrison, M., Tay, L., & Diener, E. (2020). Subjective well-being around the world: Trends and predictors across the life span. *Psychological Science, 31*(3), 293–305. https://doi.org/10.1177/0956797619898826

37 DePaulo, B. M. (2006). *Singled out: How singles are stereotyped, stigmatized, and ignored, and still live happily ever after*. St. Martin's Griffin.

38 DePaulo, B. M., & Morris, W. L. (2005). Singles in society and in science. *Psychological Inquiry, 16*(2–3), 57–83.

39 DePaulo, B. (2018). Toward a positive psychology of single life. In D. S. Dunn (Ed.), *Positive psychology: Established and emerging issues* (pp. 251–275). Routledge.

40 Judge, T. A., & Klinger, R. (2008). Job satisfaction: Subjective well-being at work. In M. Eid & R. J. Larsen (Eds.), *The science of subjective well-being* (pp. 393–413). Guilford.

41 Lucas, R. E., Clark, A. E., Georgellis, Y., & Diener, E. (2004). Unemployment alters the set point for life satisfaction. *Psychological Science, 15*(1), 8–13.

42 Diener, E., & Biswas-Diener, R. (2008). *Happiness: Unlocking the mysteries of psychological wealth*. Blackwell Publishing.

43 Diener & Biswas-Diener (2008).

44 Steel, P., Schmidt, J., & Schultz, J. (2008). Refining the relationship between personality and subjective well-being. *Psychological Bulletin, 134*(1), 138–161. https://doi.org/10.1037:0033-2909.134.1.138

45 Zhang, J. W., & Howell, R. T. (2011). Do time perspectives predict unique variance in life satisfaction beyond personality traits? *Personality and Individual Differences, 50*(2), 1261–1266. https://doi.org/10.1016/j.paid.2011.02.021

46 West, C., Mogilner, C., & DeVoe, S. E. (2021). Happiness from treating the weekend like a vacation. (2021). *Social Psychological and Personality Science, 12*(3), 346–356. https://doi.org/10.1177/1948550620916080

47 West et al. (2021).

48 Atalay, A. S., & Meloy, M. G. (2011). Retail therapy: A strategic effort to improve mood. *Psychology & Marketing, 28*(6), 638–660. https://doi.org/10.1002/mar.20404

49 Rick, S. I., Pereira, B., & Burson, K. A. (2014). The benefits of retail therapy: Making purchase decisions reduces residual sadness. *Journal of Consumer Psychology, 24*(3), 373–380. https://doi.org/10.1016/j.jcps.2013.12.004

50 Kang, M., & Johnson, K. K. P. (2011). Retail therapy: Scale development. *Clothing & Textiles Research Journal, 29*(1), 3–19. https://doi.org/10.1177/0887302X11399424

51 Kushlev, K., Heintzelman, S. J., Lutes, L. D., Wirtz, D., Kanippayoor, J. M., Leitner, D. L., & Diener, E. (2020). Does happiness improve health? Evidence from a randomized controlled trial. *Psychological Science, 53*(7), 807–821. https://doi.org/10.1177/0956797620919673

52 Diener, E., Emmons, R. A., Larsen, R. J., & Griffen, S. (1985). The Satisfaction with Life Scale. *Journal of Personality Assessment, 49*(1), 71–75.

53 Kang, M., & Johnson, K. K. P. (2011). Retail therapy: Scale development. *Clothing & Textiles Research Journal, 29*(1), 3–19. https://doi.org/10.1177/0887302X11399424

Index

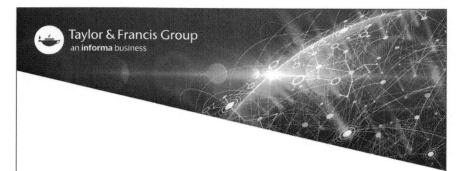